Praying
the
Bible

Finding Personal Meaning in the *Siddur*, Ending Boredom & Making Each Prayer Experience Unique

Rabbi Mark H. Levin, DHL

For People of All Faiths, All Backgrounds
JEWISH LIGHTS Publishing
Nashville, Tennessee

Praying the Bible:
Finding Personal Meaning in the Siddur, *Ending Boredom & Making Each Prayer Experience Unique*

2016 Quality Paperback Edition, First Printing
© 2016 by Mark H. Levin

Library of Congress Cataloging-in-Publication Data
Names: Levin, Mark H., 1949- author.
Title: Praying the Bible : finding personal meaning in the Siddur, ending
    boredom & making each prayer experience unique / Rabbi Mark H. Levin.
Description: Woodstock, VT : Jewish Lights Publishing, [2016] | Includes
    bibliographical references.
Identifiers: LCCN 2016024523| ISBN 9781580238694 (pbk.) | ISBN
    9781580238809 (ebook)
Subjects: LCSH: Prayer—Judaism.
Classification: LCC BM669 .L48 2016 | DDC 296.4/5—dc23 LC record available
    at https://lccn.loc.gov/2016024523

10 9 8 7 6 5 4 3 2 1

Manufactured in the United States of America
Cover Design: Tim Holtz
Cover Art: Border art, © Shutterstock/Arkady Mazor. Torah scroll, © Laurie Cate/
Flickr/Creative Commons Public License; https://creativecommons.org/licenses/
by/2.0/legalcode.
Interior Design: Tim Holtz

For People of All Faiths, All Backgrounds
Published by Jewish Lights Publishing
An imprint of Turner Publishing Company
Nashville, Tennessee
Tel: (615) 255-2665   Fax: (615) 255-5081
www.jewishlights.com
www.turnerpublishing.com

Contents

Acknowledgments

I have lived with these ideas for nearly two decades. Working with Rabbi Lawrence A. Hoffman, PhD, toward my DHL (Doctor of Hebrew Letters) afforded me the opportunity to look at the roles of Bible in our liturgy. Rabbi Hoffman's ideas of Jewish community motivated much of my congregational work, and these ideas of how the liturgy functions both on the page and in our lives inspired me to help thoughtful praying people to creatively expand their prayer lives. Rabbi Hoffman teaches that we know nothing about a prayer until we know what it means to the person who is praying. The possibility of encouraging greater meaning in the lives of those who pray has prompted this book.

Five years ago I decided that if this book were ever to be written, I would have to retire from my congregational position to complete the task. I waited three more years to retire. In those years and after, I discussed the underlying ideas of this book and some of the specific examples many times with my Shabbat morning Torah study class. All of the members have been an absolute joy to teach, and receiving their feedback on how these quotations might function in their prayer lives has moved me to expand my explorations of Bible citations in prayers. My enormous gratitude to the members of my Shabbat morning class for sticking with me all these years.

I could not have written this book or explored these ideas without the works of previous scholars. Rabbi David Abudraham, author of *Avudraham HaShalem*, of fourteenth-century Seville, Spain, was the greatest inspiration and the most complete source. He saw biblical references in a high percentage of words and phrases in the siddur, the Jewish prayer book, some of which were certainly questionable but all of which led to thoughts about the meaning of phrases in the context of a particular prayer. Rabbi Seligman Baer, author of the essential siddur *Seder Avodat Yisrael*, from Biebrich, in Wiesbaden, Germany, was an invaluable trove of ideas for the origin of words and the meanings of prayers. His exhaustive knowledge of Hebrew and the content of prayers was a constant inspiration. Cantor Macy Nulman and his truly vast, cogent, and astounding modern work *The Encyclopedia of Jewish Prayer* provided valuable clarification and references for this book and much of my work in prayer. His clarity and concise summaries provided endless help, and for those who do not read Hebrew, it's the first of these sources that you will find not only accessible but also absolutely necessary to a complete knowledge of Jewish prayer.

I am indebted again to Rabbi Lawrence A. Hoffman, PhD, for his monumental work *My People's Prayer Book*, and particularly the comments of Dr. Marc Brettler, who wrote the Bible commentary for the series. The depth of knowledge of many of the authors, beginning with Dr. Brettler, but including both Rabbi Hoffman and Dr. Joel M. Hoffman, as well as others, helped considerably through their writing with developing the thoughts portrayed in this book. All of them are much better scholars than I can ever hope to be, and I am so very grateful that they have added their devotion to prayer to the storehouse of our knowledge of the siddur.

In addition, I had the privilege of receiving the suggestions of my dear friend Jan Harness, of Overland Park, Kansas, who read much of this book. Jan's creativity, knowledge of the English language and grammar, and most importantly her constant good humor and perspective were a godsend and constant assurance during my months of writing. Everyone should have such a cheerleader to keep you moving forward toward a lifelong goal.

Stuart M. Matlins, publisher and editor in chief of Jewish Lights, changed the direction of learning and assimilating Jewish spiritual literacy in the English-speaking world. That's an enormous accomplishment, and it takes quite a while to appreciate the magnitude of his contribution. I feel fortunate that Stuart not only accepted my book but also has been very attentive to improving its style and content. His insightful comments and encouragement assured me that these ideas regarding prayer would find an appreciative audience, and motivated me to aim for intelligent and well-educated readers who have achieved a high level of excellence in their own lives and will look for a clear and innovative approach to a complex subject. Stuart has been a joy as well as a guide-post in my life.

Emily Wichland, my editor with Jewish Lights, took the rough-hewn book I produced and made it into a thing of beauty. Her close reading for style and content, her consistency and deep knowledge of the inner workings of a book, polished my creation to bring out what-ever beauty lies within. In addition, I can't imagine a nicer person to encounter as an editor. Emily made the editing experience a pure joy, and I delighted in every one of our interactions over these last months of preparation.

I am privileged to be among the last group of books published by Jewish Lights under the ownership of Stuart M. Matlins and the editing of Emily Wichland as part of it. It has been an honor to be associated with both.

How does a man thank his wife, when she is the basis of his life? None of my work would be possible without the inestimable Kacy Childs Levin, who has, for some reason I will never quite fathom but for which I thank God daily, allowed me to be her life partner. I married the kind-est and most selfless person, and Kacy creates the space in the world for me to touch other lives as much as God gives me the capacity to do so. There is no possibility of thanking her enough for making this book pos-sible, along with every other beautiful aspect of my life.

To our six children and one grandchild: Jessica and Ben, Amy, Adam, Kyle, Seth, and the scrumptious Rachel: it has taken me a life-time to integrate prayer seamlessly into my life, to rely upon and feel the presence of the Divine in nearly every moment. It has taken private work, and the willingness to honestly examine my life. But the hard work has been worth the result. I pray that you, too, will have the good fortune throughout your lives, in which you will certainly be confronted by personal trials, to have the companionship of the history and God of the Jewish people, as well as the love of family with which you have pro-vided me each and every day. This work could not have seen the light of day without the meaning you give my life.

Finally, to the members of Congregation Beth Torah, particularly the members of the Liturgical Teams over the last two decades and my Shabbat morning class members: your perspectives on prayer in general and the siddur in particular have shown me the role of prayer in modern Jewish life. Thank you, one and all, for your feedback about our worship and how it touches your lives. I had the privilege to watch you and experiment for twenty-six years; and now, in retirement, we consider it a joy to participate in the praying community of Beth Torah. May God bless your road that lies ahead.

My gratitude to all these who have guided me along the way, and the many I am sure I have left out who have touched my prayer life. Among these are my teachers of blessed memory: Rabbi Abraham Shusterman and Rabbi Eugene Lipman. I modeled my rabbinate after their examples, and no words will express clearly how much they influenced my prayer life.

To all those who taught me along the way: my gratitude is boundless. The errors in this book are most certainly my own. *Mi kol m'lamdai his'kalti*: I have tried to learn from everyone whose life path I was fortunate enough to encounter. But inevitably I sometimes err. I hope you will forgive me, and if you judge me, judge me, please, at least in part, by my intention to add a small but positive sum to the storehouse of the treasure that is the partnership between the God of Israel and those who choose to follow God's path. *V'kol netivoteha shalom*: "And all its paths are peace."

Prologue

Our Rabbis taught: Once the wicked government issued a decree forbidding the Jews to study and practice the Torah. Pappus ben Judah came and found Rabbi Akiba publicly bringing gatherings together and occupying himself with the Torah. He said to him, "Akiba, are you not afraid of the government?" He replied, "I will explain to you with a parable:

> "A fox was once walking alongside of a river, and he saw fishes going in swarms from one place to another. He said to them, 'From what are you fleeing?'
>
> "They replied, 'From the nets cast for us by men.'
>
> "He said to them, 'Would you like to come up on to the dry land so that you and I can live together in the way that my ancestors lived with your ancestors?'
>
> "They replied, 'Are you the one that they call the cleverest of animals? You are not clever but foolish. If we are afraid in the element in which we live, how much more in the element in which we would die!'
>
> "So it is with us. If such is our condition when we sit and study the Torah, of which it is written, 'For that is your life and the length of your days,' if we go and neglect it how much worse off we shall be!"
>
> (Babylonian Talmud, *Berakhot* 61b)

At first sight, the relationship between *halachah* and *agada* in prayer appears to be simple. Tradition gives us the text, we create the *kavanah*. The text is given once and for all, the inner devotion comes into being every time anew. The text is the property of all ages, *kavanah* is the creation of a single moment. The text belongs to all Jews, *kavanah* is the private concern of every individual. And yet the problem is far from being simple. The text comes out of a book, it is given; *kavanah* must come out of the heart. But is the heart always ready—three times a day—to bring forth devotion? And if it is, is its devotion in tune with what the text proclaims?

(Abraham Joshua Heschel, "No Time for Neutrality," in *Moral Grandeur and Spiritual Audacity: Essays*, ed. Susannah Heschel [New York: Farrar, Straus and Giroux, 1996], 112)

We must learn now to study the inner life of the words that fill the world of our prayerbook.... A word has a soul, and we must learn how to attain insight into its life.

(Abraham Joshua Heschel, "No Time for Neutrality," in *Moral Grandeur and Spiritual Audacity: Essays*, ed. Susannah Heschel [New York: Farrar, Straus and Giroux, 1996], 116)

Introduction

Modern Jews doubt. We are renowned for doubting. "Are you sure of that?" could well be called "the watchword of our faith" rather than the *Shema*. It's repeated often, and we are sometimes more certain of our doubts than of our beliefs.

If we doubt things that can be proved, like whether Sean and Jessica are breaking up or whether Uncle Mark is right that the Yankees were in the 1965 World Series (he's wrong; it was 1964), then we certainly doubt whether God hears prayer or even whether God exists at all. When philosopher René Descartes wrote, "*Cogito ergo sum*" (I think, therefore I am), he guaranteed that educated rationalists henceforward and forever would entertain doubt about God's existence. It's a 350-year-old story. And if we doubt God's very existence, Lord knows (oops) we doubt that the God whose existence we doubt hears prayer.

Yet, you and I crave God's guarantees. Even if Freud contended that religion is a crutch (another reason to doubt), we still yearn for the comfort an Almighty can bring. We pray not only for better algebra grades but also that those we love will love us back, that that subcutaneous lump is only a cyst, that our children arrive home safely, and that we win at fantasy football. So often we pray for results, that things will go well for us and those we love.

When I was little, my older sister wanted a Betsy Wetsy doll. When my aunt and uncle got the doll for her for Hanukkah, she told my mother, "I was a good girl; I asked for it; and I got it." So often even adults behave as though they believe this formula works, and simultaneously they doubt it. The thinking person's irresolution translates to doubting the very process that we believe prayer to be, and therefore many engage in prayer hesitantly at best.

And doubt is not the only problem with prayer. It's also boring. It's so repetitious! The same words over and over again, day after day, week after week, prayer after prayer. In some Jewish worship we might say the very same prayers two or even four times! Yipes, how much praise does this God need anyway? It's like riding a stationary bike. The wheel keeps turning, but the scenery is the same.

So the modern Jew ends up thinking, "Maybe our ancestors, in their naïveté, believed in God without any doubt and could stick it out through all of this nonsense. But, frankly, I'm doubtful and bored."

Or perhaps, our ancestors knew something we don't know.

What did they know? They knew what you, dear reader, are about to discover. They knew that Jewish prayer creates meaning in at least four or five different ways, not only literal interpretation. Jews pray poetically. The Jewish method of prayer is not simply a matter of wish fulfillment, praise of God, or thanksgiving; nor does prayer rest solely on the existence of God. Jewish prayer raises fundamental existential questions that we wrestle with daily, like "How do I deal with pain and anxiety?" and "What does my life mean?" Jewish prayer implants history, values, and stories within us, within the soul. We can call on them whenever we need them to help with our lives, like a refreshing spiritual well dug deep within to quench our longing thirst through living's inevitable heat waves and droughts. Jewish prayer takes the issues that make us most human—death, illness, loneliness, and more—and sets them in a context so that they can be handled by any person—Maimonides and Einstein or you and me.

But you, my dear friend, have likely never been taught this most complex and fundamentally rewarding aspect of prayer. So let's start in right now.

[Author's Note: You will see in the biblical quotations in each chapter that a small portion of the quotation will be in **bold**. The bold indicates either that these words are quoted in the prayer or that the theme represented by these words is the theme of the prayer that will be discussed.]

Adonai Sefatai

What Does God Want from Me Anyway?

O Lord, open my lips that my mouth may declare Your praise.[1]

Erev Shabbat worship with 200 people in our 400-seat sanctuary. As we open the *Amidah*, everyone standing, the congregation sings, "*Anananananana Adonai, Anananana sefatai tiftach ...*" I am swaying with the music, facing eastward toward the ark. Some bounce just a bit to the beat, getting into it, as our guitar, bass, and piano accompaniment for two singers fills the sanctuary with a "wall of sound." We want God to open our lips, so that we may declare God's glory, just as the opening line encourages. But why? What's this about? We're getting into the prayer mode and mood. It seems mystical, like we are uniting with God. What are we going for here?

One thing for sure: people who sing feel the exultation of prayer more keenly than those who merely recite. The sanctuary brims with enthusiasm, literally "the spirit of God." Emotions rise. God's presence throbs in the unity of the congregation tied to one another by the crescendoing music. What's the message?

Our congregation craves the exultation of a concert, but with spirituality. Worship competes in mall-centered suburbia—with movies, concerts, Friday night high school football and basketball. Fans

1

get into the activities that excite their passions. Many of our people have a much higher average weekly attendance record with the NFL than with Shabbat and God, even though the NFL only plays half the year! The last thing we want to be in worship is boring. We are in the presence of a voluntary congregation, people who have chosen to live Judaism on Erev Shabbat, and we need to keep them involved. Music will tie them together as a community, and hopefully each will also find the presence of her or his God in the room, with whom to commune spiritually.

But we don't tell them very much about God. That they must discover on their own, because each person's experience of God will differ. We let the prayer book and the singing speak for us, to give content to what people believe.

We're singing a message in code! But we don't explain that to those who are bouncing to the rhythms. They read the prayer literally: "God, open my lips to praise You!" The embedded message concerns the deepest God problem immediately following Rome's destruction of the Second Temple two thousand years ago: What does it mean that God allowed God's sanctuary to be destroyed? Is the Temple's demise a sign that God abandoned us? What about the sacrifices? For the last one thousand years the priests told us that the daily sacrifices maintain our God connection. If the sacrifices are gone, has the covenant with God gone, too? What will we do if God has cut us off? These questions are not irrelevant to the prayers in the room. We have not witnessed the destruction of God's sanctuary in Jerusalem or the cessation of sacrifice. But we certainly live in a time of profound doubt about our God link. What is the connection to God today?

We are telling one another how Jews continued to fulfill God's covenant of sacrifices, what for one thousand years we thought God wanted of us, and how we are going to fulfill God's desire today.

Immediately following the Second Temple's destruction, expectations had to radically change. The Jews asked: How can we continue to connect to God with no Jerusalem Temple? How do we solve this aching feeling of our presence and God's absence after the Temple's destruction?

Seeking Contrition, Not Sacrifice

Today those same feelings exist in a different context. Have we been cut off from God? *Adonai Sefatai*, our song, provides a concrete answer. It's also very hidden—so hidden that it's known only to a few because the worshiper needs to know and consider the second half of Psalm 51.

Let's take a look:

> **O Lord, open my lips**
> **that my mouth may declare Your praise.**
> You do not want me to bring sacrifices;
> You do not desire burnt offerings;
> True sacrifice to God is a contrite spirit;
> God, You will not despise
> a contrite and crushed heart.
>
> May it please You to make Zion prosper;
> rebuild the walls of Jerusalem.
> Then You will want sacrifices offered in
>   righteousness,
> burnt and whole offerings;
> then bulls will be offered on Your altar.
>
> (PSALM 51:17–21)

Jews believed themselves tied to God by contract, the covenant (*b'rit*). The Torah stipulates the conditions of the contract. Until Tishah B'Av, the ninth of the Hebrew month of Av, in the year 70 CE, we as a nation assumed that we maintained that pact on the Temple Mount, in Jerusalem, by offering the daily sacrifices prescribed by God and recorded in the Torah. But the day after the Roman destruction, the Temple lay flaming in ruins. Sacrifice had come to an absolute end several weeks prior. The biblical book of Deuteronomy had seven centuries earlier forbidden offering sacrifices anywhere but the Temple Mount, by the priests and in the appointed fashion. Sacrifice was done! What did these new events mean to hungry souls and insecure, defeated people?

Did God destroy God's covenant, have a second thought, let the Jewish people loose in favor of another lover?

Clearly none of that could be true, but what was the answer? How could we handle our doubts? Had God sent a replacement? Was the connection destroyed, or perhaps replaced? What did we as a people have to hold on to? Perhaps an earlier leader, one who knew God in the classic period of Jewish history, someone closer to God, might have anticipated our problem and solved it for us?

Within two decades after the Romans destroyed God's Temple, Rabban Gamaliel II provided an answer, in the form of a series of prayers. According to the Babylonian Talmud, he had Shimon HaPakuli construct eighteen blessings that would be a symbolic stand-in for the daily sacrifice, offered morning and afternoon, *shacharit* and *minchah*. Words replaced sacrifice! But how could that be? Did the Rabbis simply make this up? How to rationalize the quite obvious discontinuity, at the very least, of the nexus tying the Jewish people to God? Does this not also pose our modern question of whether our entire approach to prayer is simply a figment of our vivid and hope-filled imaginations?

You remember King David, the king who knew God and composed psalms, according to Jewish tradition, singing at midnight to God on his lyre? What could David, God's anointed quoted here, tell us about our seemingly despised situation after the Second Temple's destruction nearly a millennium before it occurred, even before Solomon built the First Temple?

David had suffered, as we'll see, and yet he survived. What did he learn about connecting to God? What could we do about the loss of our sacrifices to God? How could we survive spiritually? And by what justification might Rabban Gamaliel assert that these prayers could possibly replace the covenantal daily sacrifice?

As it turns out, according to King David in Psalm 51, God never actually required or wanted sacrifices per se! Our previous assumptions were just wrong! We had misperceived the reality of God's requirements of God's people. Now we come to realize the truth. Animal, libation, and plant sacrifice had been, although we didn't realize it earlier, a symbolic method to demonstrate to God our contrite spirit. Who knew? In

Isaiah 1 the prophet had asserted much earlier that sacrifice without good conduct was all along meaningless to God, strongly implying that sacrifice alone just wouldn't do it. God was "sated with burnt offerings of rams, suet of fatlings, and blood of bulls" (Isaiah 1:11). It wasn't that God didn't desire those things! Isaiah told Israel that sacrifice was empty without ethical conduct, and according to tradition, King David had even earlier told Israel that God really wanted a demonstration of contrition, exemplified by sacrifice.

Offering Our Humility

There's more than one way to skin this cat, according to Rabban Gamaliel. In the absence of a Temple, we can also offer the prayer of our lips and bow before God to fully display our heart's contrition. What's more, conditions have changed. God, not the people, removed the sacrifices. Therefore we have a new way: words replace sacrifices!

Let us not misconstrue David's insight here. If God should restore sacrifices in the future, we will perform them. But that will be in God's own time. When that occurs, according to God's plan, we will be only too happy to once again resume the sacrifices, as God commanded in the Torah. But now is not that time.

Fortunately, the covenantal relationship does not depend on sacrifice, but instead on what the sacrifices symbolize: a contrite spirit offered humbly to God. All great religions emphasize diminution of the ego, of the self, before a Higher Power than ourselves in order to achieve spiritual awareness. King David realized this truth early on, even before the Temple was built to God's glory. Bowing demonstrates our humbled condition, even as we immediately rise to stand before God in contrition. Humility we can provide without offering sacrifices and even enact by bowing before God with the opening words of the next prayer. When God decides, in God's wisdom, to restore the earlier system, we will be there for God as God has always been there for us. By quoting and singing or reciting from Psalm 51, we connect Judaism without sacrifice to the one thousand years of Judaism with sacrifice in a continuous, uninterrupted chain of tradition. We link our lives to King David, the direct ancestor of the messiah, and all of the biblical generations who lived in the Land of Israel and are buried there. God did not abandon us, the prayer states. The destruction of the Second Temple brought us to a higher spiritual awareness, already described by King David in Psalm 51, but we didn't notice.

All of this, in just six Hebrew words.

Adon Olam

No Lexapro or Xanax Needed

Eternal Lord who reigned supreme,
Before all beings were created,
When everything was made according to His will,
Then He was called "King."

And when all shall cease to be,
He alone will reign supreme.
He was, He is,
And He will be crowned in glory.

He is One. There is no second
To compare to Him or consort with Him.
Without beginning, without end,
Power and dominion are His.

He is my God, my living Redeemer,
My stronghold in troubled times.
He is my sign and my banner,
My cup when I call on Him.

In His hand I trust my soul
When I sleep and when I wake.

> And with my soul, my body too,
> Adonai is mine. I shall not fear.[1]

Being a boomer growing up in the 1950s and '60s, I felt like all the blessings of the world belonged inherently to me, laid in my cradle as my birthright, like Isaac's blessing of Jacob. Suddenly, after the financial limitations my parents suffered in the Great Depression and the Second World War, infinite possibility washed over America, as though God were rewarding the victors. We always had food on the table, clothing to wear, and a house I loved, with its twelve hundred square feet and one bathroom for four of us. I attended excellent, nearly all-Jewish public schools, and some summers I got to go to camp for a week. My dad went bankrupt only once, searched for and changed jobs every few years, with never more than a few months without work, and we actually took family vacations some summers.

Now in my sixties, I've enjoyed six decades of almost constant blessings. Yet, when I reflect, I realize that some anxiety frequently "couched at the door" (Genesis 4:7) ready to strike my family. Consider: my mother lost both parents before she was thirty-one and my father, orphaned from his mother at six months, lost his father at twenty-four while serving in World War II. Dad's unemployment worried my mother, whose denunciations of those infatuated by money hid her disappointment at not having more security. Mom underwent major surgery on her esophagus in 1950, suffered encephalitis in 1956, had both breasts removed in 1975, and beat metastatic ovarian cancer after surgery and chemotherapy in 1984–85. My sister married but never had children, discovered she had multiple sclerosis at age twenty-five, was permanently in a wheelchair by age thirty, lost her husband at fifty-three, and died at fifty-six. My parents, obviously, lost a daughter from whom they had no grandchildren. My brother-in-law, who predeceased his wife, had been an accomplished psychologist and devoted his extra-work life to caring for my sister. My sister, when she worked, held a social work degree and had a successful career for a decade or so.

Given my family's blessings and challenges, would you say the glass was half empty or half full? Regardless, my parents suffered plenty of angst, particularly my mother, for whom, as an only child, anxiety came with breast milk.

So why the personal biography? Because I suspect that your family's life has not been too dissimilar. In every life, moments arrive when we wonder what we did to deserve the horrible fate that we are suffering or that awaits us. Theological reflections occur naturally to all human beings. We all at times feel alone and frightened by what confronts us. Can prayer help us cope with the most difficult moments of our lives?

Adon Olam: Praying Poetry

Let us consider the vision of *Adon Olam* and see if it offers some help.

It's said that the eleventh-century Spanish Jewish prayer-poet Solomon ibn Gabirol wrote *Adon Olam*, but we're not sure. It's been used at weddings and funerals. As a child, I memorized it to conclude worship. Some congregations sing it early in daily morning worship, and some individuals recite it privately in bed at night before sleep.

At every congregation where I go to speak, every Jew in the room knows all the words by heart. Ironically, although they've memorized the poem, most Jews I know haven't the slightest idea what it means. They may never have even read a translation, let alone given some thought to how the statements fit into their lives.

We've already said, "Jews pray poetically." What does that mean? It means not only that the praying person creates the meaning, but that the interplay among your background, the composed words, and the embedded quotations creates an abundance of possible meanings, like sparks from flint striking iron!

We need a little background in the stuff you were not told about how Jewish prayer actually is intended to work! Somehow, between the time that everyday Jews really knew the Bible in Hebrew and today, we just let this go, as if somehow Jews would magically know what the prayers were intended to mean.

Poets employ single words or phrases to convey entire fields of meaning, not just one stalk but a meadow of tasseled wheat with just a phrase. By transplanting words that originally grew in other literary pastures, and thereby may be overlaid with emotional content as well, an author establishes a new hybrid as text and intertext (the quotation) collide.

Let me give you two examples: In Dr. Martin Luther King Jr.'s 1963 Lincoln Memorial speech, he ended with the Negro spiritual "Free at last, free at last, thank God almighty, I'm free at last." Dr. King's speech climaxed with those words, evoking and channeling the pent-up passions of lifetimes suffering under and struggling to be freed from Jim Crow, lifetimes singing in churches waiting for that liberation culminating before the Lincoln Memorial. Dr. King funneled all the churning emotions in memories of people who separately sang in their homes and neighborhoods about freedom and who now came together with a single voice and motive. All of that historical roiling disquiet King induced and employed in service of his cause with a single, familiar phrase.

At the opening of this chapter I commented that my childhood life seemed naturally full of blessings, "like Isaac's blessing of Jacob." I employed Jewish culture to make a point: that Isaac's undeserved blessing of Jacob has something to do with my life. That single allusion could consciously bring you, the reader, into the story of Jacob's apparent theft of his brother Esau's blessing. The blessing sat uneasily with Jacob, and Esau became outraged. In what sense might I have evoked that biblical scene to describe my own life? In what sense were the blessings I enjoyed passed on to me by my parents, as Isaac's blessing was to Jacob? What blessings might I feel I have stolen from someone for whom they were meant, like my older, firstborn sister? Even as I intended the phrase to draw you into Jewish culture, I also intended you to ask yourself these and other questions, all from a simple allusion to a very Jewish, biblical story. We will see that Jewish prayers utilize this same technique constantly.

But let's start by interpreting the opening of *Adon Olam*.

"Eternal Lord Who Reigned Supreme": Infinite God Beyond Time or Space

The first two words, *Adon olam*, is a pun, meaning either "eternal Master/ Lord" or "Master/Lord of the world." With just two words, the poet fixes in our minds that God rules over time and space, with no division between the two, as the same term denotes both. Immediately we are challenged in our idea of God. God reigns because God alone extends through all eternity and space without companion or peer. Before and after all creation, in every place and time, God rules unchallenged. This is the view of an almighty God we most likely were taught in childhood.

Having established God's absolute dominance and uniqueness across all dimensions, the poet turns to applying that Reality in the reader's personal life. This ultimate Controller of all cares about us as individuals, "little ole me," this self I call home. Do you remember Paul Simon's song "You Can Call Me Al"? "If you'll be my bodyguard, I can be your long lost pal." Having just described the Sole Bodyguard, the Ultimate Sovereign, the poet now claims that Sovereign as his Redeemer. That's protection! That's comfort. There is no escaping God; as a Parent/ Protector, God's presence enfolds our lives. Is God eternal and omnipresent, or more limited? What do you believe? How does God's eternity fit into your world? For me, acknowledging the gnawing internal ache of my own mortality, I connect positively with my presence in God's eternity. That reality helps me feel that not only am I not alone in this life, but also that something of me continues after my own death in God's eternal existence. This God is *my* God and Protector.

"He Is My God, My Living Redeemer": The God of Job

Now Ibn Gabirol turns to allusion in the fourth stanza, exploiting just a two-word quotation: *v'chai goali*, "my living Redeemer"! What context is Ibn Gabirol evoking? The iconic sufferer, Job. The greatest Power in the universe protects *me*!

Why do I need protection? Because I have problems and enemies both within and without. Job suffers as no other human being. First, he endures punishment for no earthly reason. He is the butt of a bet between God and an angelic adversary, HaSatan. Talk about feeling persecuted by unseen forces in the universe! Who expects God to get on their case without cause? What anguish! God persecutes Job on purpose. At least we don't claim that distinction.

Job raises a deeper question. He is stricken not in spite of but precisely because he is righteous. It's the characterization of life as absurd and a challenge to God's goodness. If I suffer as Job does, how can the world possibly be a fair place? Should I simply despair? Consider the story: Job is a totally innocent and virtuous man whom the Adversary (HaSatan—an angel in God's entourage) claims will turn against God should his life turn and his blessings cease. So they bet, and God causes Job to lose the big three blessings: wealth, family, and personal health. Truth is hidden from Job by God Himself! Job has no possibility of comprehending why he suffers so. But, then, neither do we ultimately know why we suffer. Job's just an extreme case. But Job knows with perfect faith that his suffering is not a result of his sins, as the biblical book of Deuteronomy implies: "I place before you this day life and death, blessing and the curse. Therefore choose life, and you and your children may live" (Deuteronomy 30:19). Somehow, even though Job doesn't see the whole picture, he has faith that if he did, it would make sense.

Throughout my decades as a rabbi, people have asked why tragedy occurred in their lives. They simply wanted to know what they had done to cause their suffering. *Adon Olam* makes three points clear: we can't know, sometimes we suffer even though we've been good people, and God remains our Protector even through our anguish.

Job's three friends come to comfort him but end up accusing him and increasing his pain. They unjustly conclude, with zero evidence and armed only with their erroneous theological assumptions, that his ailments are due to sin. They instruct him to repent so that God will remove his suffering. God relieve us of such friends, who force their theological assumptions on us and increase rather than assuage our pain!

But Job will not relent and relinquish his truth. He will neither abandon God nor believe that God has forsaken him. He knows for certain that his Redeemer lives, although he cannot comprehend the source of his suffering. In other words: even if we can't see the big picture, life does make sense in an ultimately meaningful way.

That Redeemer is the infinite God the poet describes. And so I can say, as the person praying, that the all-powerful God protects me as I now stand in Job's position. I am suffering not because of my sins, but despite the fact that I do not deserve this pain. However, if Job can endure his losses and survive despite the injustice of loss, then, I may conclude, so can I! God grants me, as God does to Job, the strength and insight to endure through my faith in the orderliness and meaningfulness of God's world. Job endures so much worse. Certainly I can absorb and live with my incomprehensible losses if Job can overcome his.

All this in just two words, one quotation (*v'chai goali*)! I find comfort that others have walked a similar life path and gained the insights to triumph over pain, both physical and mental. Since Job suffers the three great calamities, loss of wealth, children, and health, how much better off must I be? With just two brief words, I am assured that just as Job not only withstands his ailments but also, at the end of the book, receives a reward with the return of his wealth, family, and health, so my suffering may be rewarded as well. At the very least I will gain more insight because of my struggles, and appreciate the blessings in my life that much more. I not only dip within to drink from the well, but there are also moments when the well simply offers itself to me. This is not a promise that I will be returned to my pre-loss state of affairs. Rather, that with God's justice, I may find rewards commensurate to my good deeds. But surely, regardless of the outcome, God has implanted within me the capacity to endure and discover blessing, even in misfortune! Just as Job withstands defeat, so will I.

"My Stronghold in Troubled Times": The God of King David

The theme established by the story of Job continues in the next verse, *V'tzur chevli b'eit tzarah*, "My stronghold in troubled times," utilizing David's Psalm 18. David thanks God for saving him from his enemy, King Saul, before David assumed the throne.

> For the leader. Of David, the servant of Adonai, who addressed the words of this song to Adonai after Adonai saved him from the hands of all his enemies and from the clutches of Saul....

Ropes of Death encompassed me;
torrents of Belial terrified me;
ropes of Sheol encircled me;
snares of Death confronted me.
In my distress I called on Adonai,
cried out to my God;
in His temple He heard my voice;
my cry to Him reached His ears....

Adonai rewarded me according to my merit;
He requited the cleanness of my hands;
for I have kept to the ways of Adonai,
and have not been guilty before my God;
for I am mindful of all His rules;
I have not disregarded His laws.
I have been blameless toward Him,
and have guarded myself against sinning;
and Adonai has requited me according to my merit,
the cleanness of my hands in His sight.
With the loyal, You deal loyally;
with the blameless man, blamelessly.

(PSALM 18:1, 18:5–7, 18:21–26)

David calls upon God in his distress, just as we may be doing when praying. He had been unjustly attacked, both by the jealous King Saul and later by his own upstart son, Absalom. Unjustified misfortune can be so frustrating! As if in a distant mirror, we see our lives reflected in David's. Saul's insane jealousy caused him to attack David both verbally and physically. Absalom's anger with his father after his sister, Tamar, was raped by their half-brother, Amnon, and Absalom's overwhelming ambition goaded him to attempt to violently seize the throne. These are the ropes that encircled David. But the threats failed. Was it David's cunning or his favor in God's eyes that enabled him to circumvent misfortune? Clearly, David believed that without God no one can triumph. Yet, all accounts praise David's warrior skills. Perhaps it is true, as the psalmist tells us, that ultimately those who keep God's commandments will receive reward, even if along the way they suffer hardship.

The Hebrew for the verse in *Adon Olam* "My stronghold in troubled times," *V'tzur* [Psalm 89:44] *chevli* [Psalm 18:5] *b'eit tzarah*, literally means "Blade of my ropes in time of trouble." In other words, God is the blade that cuts through the ropes binding King David, and God can be the blade that cuts the ropes binding me as well.

"Isn't that my story, too?" we ask ourselves. Haven't I done the right thing for the most part and nonetheless suffered? How badly have I sinned? Was David that much better than me, or was he worse? Will I then receive my reward as David did? David's life, like ours, was neither guilt- nor pain-free. He committed adultery with Bathsheba and set up the death of her husband, Uriah the Hittite. As a result, God punished him, according to the biblical book of Second Samuel. David lost the offspring of his adultery to illness. David himself died weak and in pain. Yet, David triumphed over his ills, passing his kingdom on to Bathsheba and his son Solomon in a poignant deathbed scene of doing the right thing for the prophet Nathan, Bathsheba, and Solomon together. Physical weakness does not mean defeat and can be momentarily overcome. It may be our fate, particularly later in life if we live long enough, but it does not signal failure, and opportunities for success will come our way, as they did for David.

Beginning in Psalm 18:21 ("The Lord rewarded me according to my merit ..."), we feel as though we could be listening to Job again, as David, too, protests his innocence and declares his faith that God will reward the righteous and punish only those who sin. Do we, too, feel ensnared by ropes in our times of trouble? But, perhaps there's a tone of moderation. David will be rewarded according to his merit and his sins. We are emphasizing that although suffering may attack any of us, we are not unique. Why then should we not suffer if they did? And yet, in reading of their lives, we also find that they overcame their suffering and God restored them.

"He Is My Sign and My Banner": The God of Moses

What about Moses, God's favorite? Before he died on 7 Adar, his 120th birthday, the Torah tells us that "his eyes were not dimmed neither was his strength abated" (Deuteronomy 34:7). Yet, Moses, too, passed through tough times while leading his people in the wilderness.

> Amalek came and fought with Israel at Rephidim. Moses said to Joshua, "Pick some men for us, and go out and do battle with Amalek. Tomorrow I will station myself on the top of the hill, with the rod of God in my hand." Joshua did as Moses told him and fought with Amalek, while Moses, Aaron, and Hur went up to the top of the hill. Then, whenever Moses held up his hand, Israel prevailed; but whenever he let down his hand, Amalek prevailed....
> Then Adonai said to Moses, "Inscribe this in a document as a reminder, and read it aloud to Joshua: I will utterly blot out the memory of Amalek from under heaven!" And Moses built an altar and named it **Adonai-nissi [Adonai is my banner]. He said, "It means, 'Hand upon the throne of Adonai!'** Adonai will be at war with Amalek throughout the ages."
>
> (Exodus 17:8–11, 17:14–16)

In Jewish lore Haman and Hitler descend from Amalek, archetypal enemy of the Jewish people. Amalek cut off the stragglers, the elderly, and the weak as we Hebrews traveled through the Sinai desert. This verse of *Adon Olam* taken from the Amalek story reminds us that God will vanquish God's enemies, the foes of God's people. We can trust that we will ultimately overcome the anti-Semites who threaten us.

When we as a people feel threatened, *Adon Olam* is the perfect song to sing to unite us and remind ourselves that we have prevailed in the past.

"My Cup When I Call on Him": The God of Psalm 23

Psalms have provided the Jewish people with spiritual solace for at least twenty-five hundred years, none more than Psalm 23. Like listening to jazz or blues, when we read a psalm we feel internally what the author felt when he stood in our shoes (or perhaps in our sandals). The psalmist transmits his internal state.

When I was a child in the 1950s, until the self-proclaimed atheist Madeline Murray (who later became Madeline Murray O'Hare) successfully campaigned for removing Bible readings and class prayer from public schools, morning class daily began with the recitation of Psalm 23 in school, along with the Lord's Prayer and the Pledge of Allegiance. Therefore, many people about my age still know Psalm 23 by heart.

Two of the most famous phrases in the psalm are "the valley of the shadow of death" and "my cup runneth over." If you asked many people, "Do you know a place where the phrase 'my cup' appears in the Bible?" if they didn't panic they'd say, "Yeah, I don't know where it's from, but isn't there something like 'my cup runneth over'?"

What does Ibn Gabirol mean by "My cup when I call on Him"? To make sense of this verse from *Adon Olam*, let's read the old translation of Psalm 23, the way I heard it in elementary school:

> The Lord is my Shepherd; I shall not want.
> He maketh me to lie down in green pastures;
> He leadeth me beside the still waters;
> He restoreth my soul.
> He guideth me in straight paths for His name's sake.
> Yea, though I walk through the Valley of the Shadow
>   of Death,
> I will fear no evil.
> For Thou art with me.
> Thy rod and thy staff they comfort me.
> Thou preparest a table before me in the presence of
>   mine enemies.
> Thou hast anointed my head with oil.
> **My cup runneth over.**
> Surely goodness and mercy shall follow me all the
>   days of my life.
> And I shall dwell in the house of the Lord forever.

God provides overwhelmingly, even when enemies assail us. We can sit calmly at the table, anointed and sated, drinking our fill, trusting in God's protection. All of this becomes possible because God cares for me the way a shepherd cares for his flock, watching over every individual sheep and making all of them God's personal concern.

I have myself been comforted by a famous midrash about Moses at Mount Sinai immediately before witnessing the burning bush. The midrash is so famous it was actually included in the classic Cecil B. DeMille movie *The Ten Commandments*, starring Charlton Heston. The Torah tells us in Exodus 3:1 that Moses was a shepherd, tending the flocks of his father-in-law, Jethro. The midrash adds detail to the story by describing how immediately before sighting the "unconsumed bush," Moses chased after a lamb that had strayed up the mountainside and gotten lost. Witnessing Moses returning down the mountain with the errant lamb in his arms, imitating God's concern for every single, unprotected creature, God understood that this humble shepherd should be chosen as the redeemer of God's people.

In Psalm 16:5 we again find not only the same image, but also the direct quotation that God is "my portion and my cup," which is then followed by "You control my fate." Not only does God watch over me, but God also controls the outcome.

Of course, this idea of controlling fate is tricky business; bad things do, after all, occur, and to some very good people. But many nonetheless find comfort in the guarantee that it is God in control, and whatever outcome ensues we at least have that satisfaction.

"In His Hand I Trust My Soul": The God of Psalm 31

The verse "In His hand I trust my soul" directly quotes Psalm 31:6:

> For You are my rock and my fortress;
> You lead me and guide me as befits Your name.
> You free me from the net laid for me,
> for You are my stronghold.

Into Your hand I entrust my spirit;
You redeem me, Adonai, faithful God.

(PSALM 31:4–6)

The writer here clearly suffers physically, struck by repulsive bodily illness, as we see beginning in verse 10:

Have mercy on me, Adonai, for I am in distress;
my eyes are wasted by vexation,
my substance and body too.
My life is spent in sorrow,
my years in groaning;
my strength fails because of my iniquity,
my limbs waste away.
Because of all my foes
I am the particular butt of my neighbors,
a horror to my friends;
those who see me on the street avoid me.
I am put out of mind like the dead;
I am like an object given up for lost.
I hear the whisperings of many,
intrigue on every side,
as they scheme together against me,
plotting to take my life.

(PSALM 31:10–14)

How many times as a congregational rabbi have I heard this story! A community member becomes ill, and over time her friends disappear, she feels abandoned and alone. The sufferer finds herself searching desperately not only for physical comfort, but for spiritual solace as well. God becomes her refuge, an umbrella, hat, and raincoat in the thunderstorm.

But I trust in You, Adonai;
I say, "You are my God!"
My fate is in Your hand;

save me from the hand of my enemies and pursuers.
Show favor to Your servant;
as You are faithful, deliver me.
Adonai, let me not be disappointed when I call You;
let the wicked be disappointed;
let them be silenced in Sheol;
let lying lips be stilled that speak haughtily against
   the righteous
with arrogance and contempt.

(PSALM 31:15–19)

Clearly this plea comes from a "typically" righteous person, who nonetheless admits her "iniquity" but does not consider herself wicked. Like many who suffer physical afflictions in our own day, she experiences not only the pain of illness but also the social isolation that too often accompanies it. That isolation need not stem from something abhorrent, a medical ailment that disgusts those around us, like diarrhea or a protruding growth. Rather, many in biblical times and in our own day find that in their illness they become less interesting to their friends and sometimes family as well. Perhaps their friends unconsciously feel the illness is contagious and want to avoid the discomfort of being around a victim. The author of the psalm suffers physically, but also psychologically, "the butt of [her] neighbors and a horror to [her] friends." Yet, she finds refuge and comfort in the presence of the Eternal One of Israel. She, too, asks for justice, that the wicked not prosper, which would mock those who have curbed their appetites in order to live moral lives. Have we not all felt this way? And here, by implication in *Adon Olam*, we find our heartfelt sentiments and silent heartache validated.

"When I Sleep and When I Wake": The God of Daniel

The final statement of belief in *Adon Olam* comes with an absolute declaration of faith in God's protection, both while we sleep and while we are awake, in this life and the next.

The Rabbis affirm resurrection of the dead to a new life. But although the Rabbis found resurrection in many places in the Bible, its actual appearance in terms of the intention of the biblical authors is unique. That appearance comes in the book of Daniel:

> At that time the great prince, Michael, who stands beside the sons of your people, will appear. It will be a time of trouble, the like of which has never been since the nation came into being. At that time, your people will be rescued, all who are found inscribed in the book. Many of those that sleep in the dust of the earth shall awake, some to eternal life, others to reproaches, to everlasting abhorrence.
> (Daniel 12:1–2) (See "Singing in the Rain" in chapter 4)

Daniel concludes with a vision of the coming of the end-times, when the dead will be resurrected, the wicked punished, and the righteous rewarded.

Judaism posits three types of resurrection: in the spring of the year when nature returns to life; in the morning when our souls are returned to our bodies after sleep; and at the end of times, with resurrection of the body and reunification with the soul. Most liberal Jews believe in the first, but not necessarily in the second and third. We understand the spring renewal of nature as a natural process. But resurrection from the grave is supernatural, defying our logic. Therefore we may not believe in the third option, although increasingly I find those who believe not only in afterlife but in reincarnation as well. *Adon Olam* concludes with the complete affirmation that we so hope in God that we place our souls in God's absolute trust: awake and asleep, alive and dead.

"Adonai Is Mine. I Shall Not Fear": The God of Psalm 118

Adon Olam concludes building on the God it describes from the outset: the absolute Sovereign of the universe, whom I claim as my God who cares directly about me. I shall fear nothing, because this providential

Sovereign will care for me, just as God cared for Moses, David, and Job. The ills that strike me can hardly be compared with theirs, and yet they were redeemed and restored to wholeness. If it can happen to them, under God's watchful eye, then certainly I may well share their fate.

> In distress I called on Adonai;
> Adonai answered me and brought me relief.
> **Adonai is on my side,**
> **I have no fear;**
> what can man do to me?
> With Adonai on my side as my helper,
> I will see the downfall of my foes.
>
> (PSALM 118:5–7)

The journey is complete. In this life and the next, whatever my circumstances, I am safe. No need for Lexapro or Xanax. Nothing need cause me existential anxiety. The all-knowing, all-seeing God has a plan that includes me. My life is part of the greater picture of the universe, and others have walked this same path, finding meaning in their lives, even though they suffered. Even Job ultimately was rewarded for his faith. Why would it be any different with me? And if Job, David, and Moses can stand their travails, why not me, who suffers so much less?

All of this, in a sung prayer/poem you may very well have known by heart for years. But you didn't realize its lessons because even if you read the translation from the Hebrew, no one ever showed you how and why the author included biblical quotations to fully illustrate his points.

And there are many more lessons if we examine the original intentions of the authors of our prayers.

Avot: Ancestors

My Grandparents
Were Great People

Blessed are You, Adonai, our God, and our ancestors' God: Abraham's God, Isaac's God, and Jacob's God, great, mighty, and revered God, supreme God, who acts most piously, who is Master of everything, who remembers the piety of our ancestors, and who brings a redeemer to their descendants for the sake of His name in love. Our King helps and saves and protects! Blessed are You, Adonai, Abraham's Protector.[1]

"Jews don't bow down to anyone but God." So I've been told my entire life, particularly in childhood. Maybe you heard it, too. Mordecai wouldn't bow to Haman. Hannah's seven sons chose execution rather than bow to Antiochus. The seventh son died refusing to pick up a coin off the floor before the king to avoid giving the wrong impression of obeisance! When I first heard that story I was filled with dread. Could I be that loyal? Suppose I was called! If Hannah's seven sons died rather than bow, we really, really don't bow before anyone but God! We dress up at Purim and wipe out Haman's name with *gragers* and screaming noise. We won, so we must have been right, I concluded. Jews worship only God. Bowing showcases obedience; so Jews bow only to the one God.

Bowing is nonverbal prayer, modeling our relationship in synagogue so that we can live our relationship outside of synagogue. We say, "Adonai, open my lips that my mouth may declare Your praise," and we bow while praying, "Blessed / are You / Adonai" (*Barukh atah Adonai*)—three movements to the bow corresponding to three Hebrew words. And according to Psalm 51, we reveal before God our contrite spirit, then rise to stand as near equals in God's eyes, because "God lifts up the fallen" (Psalm 146:8).

Jewish prayer expresses complex meanings through intricate symbolic structures, like a poem or a piece of art. Now we are beginning to look at a series of prayers that goes by three names: the *Amidah* (meaning "standing," thus the "Standing Prayer"); *HaTefilah*, or the *Tefilah* ("The Prayer," par excellence); and the *Shemoneh Esrei* ("eighteen," because it was originally eighteen prayers, now nineteen, composed as a single unit). Together these prayers substitute for the morning and afternoon sacrifices offered at the First and Second Temples on behalf of the collective Jewish people, maintaining our God covenant.

When Jews talk to God, it's called prayer. When God talks to Jews, we call it revelation. Like lovers pursuing one another, both conversations are necessary but fraught with peril. Who's really on the other side? Is there anything to discuss? How do humans communicate with the "Wholly Other"? What's our common language?

When a loving couple lacking a shared language strive to communicate verbally (think romantic comedy shows here), each attempts to find the language of the beloved. So it is with us and God. God speaks by human methods (words), and humans speak God-talk (Bible quotations).

Now, with the *Tefilah*, we answer a major issue: what do you do when your world fractures and your ground of being collapses beneath you?

God Loves Words

For one thousand years Jews connected with God through sacrifices. After Babylonia's King Nebuchadnezzar destroyed the First Temple and thrust Jews into exile, Cyrus of Persia sent us back to build the Second

Temple to offer sacrifices and reconstruct our God nexus. But after the Roman destruction of the Second Temple on Tishah B'Av (ninth of the Hebrew month of Av) in 70 CE, no more sacrifices. No third Temple. No relying on God. What happened to the Protector of Abraham, Isaac, Jacob, and their descendants?

The full story is as complicated as a Chekhov play. But, simply put, the Rabbis made prayer the core of the solution. Once a year each adult Jew had paid a half shekel tax, and thereby every day, morning and afternoon, a sacrifice, called the *tamid* (meaning "continuous," like *ner tamid*, the eternal light), was offered to God on behalf of the whole House of Israel. But now what?

Like a trapeze artist with a fraying rope, the Rabbis needed a new swing to hold them aloft, preferably one already proved safe. They chose prayer. In chapter 1 we saw the first replacement rope on the swing: the Rabbis claimed God didn't actually want sacrifice! So what were we doing those one thousand years of the First and Second Temples if not sacrificing to God? We discovered that King David (traditionally credited as author of Psalms but not historically) told us that God actually desired a contrite spirit rather than sacrifices. Sacrifice could prove contrition, but bowing and words would do it, also. So, since sacrifices are no longer available, we'll turn to the other option: prayer with bowing!

And the second replacement rope? Recite the prayers at the times that psalms were sung for half a millennium by the Levitical priests adjacent to Temple Mount sacrifices. Simultaneously, other Levites had been singing the same psalms in selected villages around Israel: at the hour of the sacrifices, *shacharit* and *minchah*, sunup and mid-afternoon. So they embraced a precedent for those times.

But what to say without the sacrifices? Speak to God in language that God uses and therefore recognizes. If God originally composed these biblical words, perhaps they even have meaning beyond our incomplete human comprehension.

Massive changes took place in Judaism in the first and second centuries CE. Continuity, or at least the appearance of continuity, was essential. For the sake of stability, we humans need roots in the past that help us withstand the storms of the present and guide us into the future.

If prayer were to replace sacrifices, how many times a day should Jews pray? Take a look at the book of Daniel:

> When Daniel learned that it had been put in writing, he went to his house, in whose upper chamber he had had windows made facing Jerusalem, *and three times a day he knelt down, prayed, and made confession to his God*, as he had always done.
>
> (Daniel 6:11; emphasis mine)

Remember Daniel in the lions' den? This is that story! Daniel's God saves him from the death sentence because of Daniel's extraordinary piety. Prayer saved Daniel! When the king witnesses what happened, that Daniel survived his enemies and the lions, he has Daniel's persecutors fed to the very lions they intended to gnaw on Daniel's bones, and the entire kingdom is instructed to worship Daniel's God. If God rewards righteousness and prayer with salvation from lions' mouths, shouldn't we follow suit and worship three times daily also? We'll see other explanations for thrice daily Jewish prayer. But, here's a biblical precedent. Apparently, the Rabbis could conclude, it works! But that's an important question for us today. Does prayer work, and how? Must prayer work supernaturally?

The *Shema* was commanded morning and evening (Deuteronomy 6:7), yielding two daily prayer times. The *Tefilah* replaced the morning and afternoon daily sacrifices, adding an afternoon prayer time. Perhaps heeding Daniel's thrice daily prayers, the *Tefilah* was extended into a third, evening, repetition, accompanying the *Shema* and Its Blessings, with the Talmudic rationale that the sacrifices burned on the altar all night so there should be a third *Tefilah* recitation. Daniel's prayer practice cleared the path forward for three daily prayer times, rooting them in history.

"God and Our Ancestors' God": The Call to Connect

We've already introduced the recitation of the entire *Tefilah*, all nineteen prayers, with the quotation from Psalm 51:17, "Adonai, open my lips that my mouth may declare your praise." But each individual prayer, besides being part of replacing the daily sacrifices and proving contrition, possesses its own, specific meaning. The first prayer, the *Avot* (literally, "Fathers"), begins, "Blessed are You, Adonai, our God, and our ancestors' God: Abraham's God, Isaac's God, and Jacob's God."

Our prayer calls on God to remember us because of our ancestors, whom God championed. I had a "burning bush moment" in my life, sometime within a year of my bar mitzvah, under the aluminum dome of Har Sinai Temple in Baltimore, during the nearly vacant afternoon worship on Yom Kippur, sitting among approximately forty prayerful souls in a vast two-thousand-chair High Holy Day expanded sanctuary. I suddenly felt a descending flow of peace, like a clear liquid, cylindrical stream the diameter of my body, washing downward from above, entering my body, leaving me with utter tranquility and a calming sensation of the coherence and absolute meaning of the world. My existential angst, my adolescent persistent worry about school and girls and my place among peers, vanished, and I sat alone but assured with the calm that everything in my world would be just fine.

When I tell the story to Christian ministers they say, "Oh, that was when you were called by God!" I wonder if you have had such a moment of divine presence. I know not everyone does. But Moses did, and we are his people. Apparently these things quietly happen to many people.

Let's read Exodus 3:4–6:

> When Adonai saw that he had turned aside to look, God called to him out of the bush: "Moses! Moses!" He answered, "Here I am." And He said, "Do not come closer. Remove your sandals from your feet, for the place on which you stand is holy ground. I am," He said, "the God of your father, **the God of Abraham, the God of Isaac, and the God of Jacob.**" And Moses hid his face, for he was afraid to look at God.

The Bible contains multiple stories of the call of a prophet to service (e.g., Isaiah 6, Jeremiah 1, Jonah 1). Here we witness Moses's call from amid a burning bush. The Torah associates Moses, the prophet of the

Exodus, with Abraham, the patriarch with whom God first established the covenant. In Genesis 15:13–15, Abraham was foretold the four-hundred-year slavery to engulf his people subsequent to his great-grandchildren's famine-induced descent into Egypt. Abraham and Moses bookend enslavement and redemption.

"Great, Mighty, and Revered God": Seeking a Spiritual World of Meaning

This redeeming God we describe as "great, mighty, and revered." But why those adjectives? Why not others? Because in the seventh century BCE Deuteronomy 10:17 described God this way, and then two centuries later the Jewish messenger Nehemiah set the precedent by quoting them in his prayer. But not only that, Nehemiah's prayer feels as though it may as well have been composed for the *Tefilah*, it is so apt to the Jews' second-century-CE circumstances:

> And now, our God, **great, mighty, and revered God**, who stays faithful to His covenant, do not treat lightly all the suffering that has overtaken us ... from the time of the Assyrian kings to this day. Surely You are in the right with respect to all that has come upon us, for You have acted faithfully, and we have been wicked. Our kings, officers, priests, and fathers did not follow Your teaching, and did not listen to Your commandments or to the warnings that You gave them. When they had their own kings and enjoyed the good that You lavished upon them, and the broad and rich land that You put at their disposal, they would not serve You, and did not turn from their wicked deeds. Today we are slaves, and the Land that You gave our fathers to enjoy its fruit and bounty—here we are slaves on it! On account of our sins it yields its abundant crops to kings whom You have set over us. They rule over our bodies and our beasts as they please, and we are in great distress.
>
> (Nehemiah 9:32–37)

In other words, through our covenant, our contract between God and Abraham for all generations, God makes prosperity on the Land possible. We ignored the contract until we blundered headfirst into persecution!

Even in our day we ask ourselves what we have done wrong in God's eyes when misfortune befalls us. Our lives are in some fashion connected to God's plan for history. As we said earlier, most of us had college professors who taught the irrationality of God belief because it assumes a spiritual existence, non-replicable and by definition unscientific. But, if there's no God, what is there about some moments that we feel as though they touch eternity? Without a higher, creative Power, the world becomes banal, continuous sameness, and we muddle through each day as best we can, with no hope of ultimacy, building into our lives sometimes more high-minded but often trivial activities that make us feel a little better about our barren existence.

Our ancestors realized that altruism—giving to others selflessly—plus love and beauty all disconnect us from our time-bound world and attach our lives to sensations of meaningfulness. Even picking up and trashing a scrap of litter from the ground for which we were not responsible improves our mood and makes us feel better about ourselves, like we have accomplished something astonishingly good and consequential. That such trivial kindness can feel so good is nothing short of astounding! Facebook is full of YouTube videos about beauty or animal harmony (think kittens here, or animals who are natural enemies playing with one another, like a panther and a goat or dogs and cats) and gratuitous acts of kindness. Warm and fuzzy movies that "pay it forward" evoke tears because they drill down into the serotonin emotion of tranquility that enables us to touch eternity. But so many of us were educated to discredit that the Eternal even exists, so we discount or even deny the transcendent feeling, even, amazingly, when we have personally experienced it. We so often fight against the purpose of prayer, even when the prayer experience itself is successful in connecting us to God.

I have seen this so often. People attend worship and for a few seconds connect to an unanticipated and inexplicably holy moment, exalting their spirits in an unguarded encounter. Then they leave the sanctuary and desacralize it through analysis, forgetting that the whole is greater than the sum of its parts. They label it a mirage in the meaning desert of their lives. It's that doubt taking over, the tyranny of skepticism ingrained in college that they never overthrew. I've had forty-five-year-old people tell me, "The rabbi yelled at me during my bar mitzvah training, so I never went back!" Really? One old guy yelled at you once three decades ago and you're letting that prevent you from touching the eternal mystery of the universe? You've given a lot of power to someone you didn't even like and barely knew.

In the second century CE once again the Land of Israel had been occupied by foreign powers and the people subjugated. But what is the cause of our disruption from God today? Then it was persecution. Today it is the seductions of affluence's allure. Money shifts our focus to prevent penetrating deeper and concentrating on God's presence through living for a higher purpose. Yet, we remain existentially malcontent, feeling that "there must be more." We invest hours staring at screens or lusting after physical satisfactions, like dogs lapping at their drinking bowls. I watch very good people idolize personal achievements: physicality, bank accounts and their blandishments. We amuse ourselves rather than connect to an external source of genuinely eternal satisfactions, like self-denying loving or sacrificial giving. When have you given your all for someone you love, without any desire or even hope for repayment? Rabbi Lawrence Kushner describes love as the night he went out in a blinding New England snow-storm searching motel candy machines for the precise candy bar his preg-nant wife just had to have! When have you gifted to someone something precious to you, that you might even miss, but that you wanted the other to possess? The physical sacrifices of altruism are spiritually rewarded.

So often the few times we connect to a higher realm we discount it into oblivion, reducing a selfless event to its physical components and rejecting the connection to a spiritual realm because we deny its exis-tence, not because we don't feel its presence. Therefore, we suffer even as our ancestors did: they because of physical enslavement, we from spiritual enslavement.

We humans come preprogrammed to respond first to our own needs. But should we not appreciate that our blessings are not solely the result of our own efforts? President Obama got into a huge uproar because he contended that no one is self-made, that we all stand on the shoulders of previous generations and enjoy the benefit of the others' work. Our self-absorbed insulation has isolated us. Here's the result: we are once again enslaved, but now it's self-inflicted. We are slaves to a purely material reality, no ultimacy to redeem us from its monotony. We do believe in love, but without a spiritual belief it too has become so physical that even sexual relations, the ultimate intimacy, are reduced to good sensations rather than the holiness of selfless devotion to a single beloved and the merger of two selves into a single beating heart. What a tragic state we've condemned ourselves to: closeted in a material world with amusements and titillating sensations to relieve the boredom rather than living in a spiritual world of meaning.

We do overcome the physical to experience extraordinary moments: a birth, a death, overwhelming natural beauty like mountaintops and Grand Canyons. These cut to our marrow, our *kishkes* (guts), as we used to say. Have you had moments that felt eternal? Do you observe them to attempt to repeat them? During my special moment in that sanctuary I was given the gift, a lifelong memory and ray of light, to viscerally realize I lived within a discoverable divine order with hierarchies of meaning. The fortunate among us dedicate our lives to uncovering and participating in that order: listening attentively to broken hearts and souls, healing living beings, salving suffering through friendship and personal presence, forging constructive connections, cathecting eternity by repairing the world, influencing our environs beyond our brief earthly sojourns. Most of us fail to structure our day-to-day life to create and then savor eternal moments, so caught up are we in the time-bound financial, status, and power pursuits of our day.

There's a power in opening the *Tefilah* with connection to ancestry, and it all started with Nehemiah twenty-four hundred years ago. We encounter a sense of our timeless qualities and the values that will give substance to our lives.

"Supreme God": Living in Harmony with God's World

Immediately following the adjectives "great, mighty, and revered," God is called *El Elyon*, "supreme God." Given the entirely Israelite description from Deuteronomy and Nehemiah, we find a startling departure. The term originates in Genesis not with a Jewish sage, but with Melchizedek, king of Salem, who was a priest of *El Elyon*. Melchizedek blesses Abram and introduces God Most High:

> Blessed be Abram of **God Most High [*El Elyon*]**,
> **Creator of heaven and earth.**
> **And blessed be God Most High,**
> Who has delivered your foes into your hand.
>
> (GENESIS 14:19)

Not only does *El Elyon* appear here as God's name, applied again by Abram in verse 22, but the next words in Hebrew are *koneh shamayim va'aretz*, "Possessor/Creator of heaven and earth." The *Avot* prayer immediately quotes a word of this next phrase as well, calling God *koneh hakol*, "Master of everything."

Melchizedek, apparently the priest/king of Salem, which for the Rabbis was the holy city of Jerusalem, introduces Abram to God Most High, one of God's names. It's difficult to ignore the universal flavor of the passage. Just as Moses will later be introduced to God on Mount Sinai by his Midianite priest father-in-law, Jethro, so Abram encounters a monotheistic non-Jewish priest, on familiar terms with the one God of all the world.

The name reappears in Psalm 78, a complete history of Israel in which Israel's close relationship and betrayal of God are thoroughly revisited. The psalm recounts the Israelites' history with and rebellion against God. But the verse recalled by the phrase "God Most High" is, happily, "They remembered that God was their rock, God Most High, their Redeemer" (Psalm 78:35).

Remember that in this post-destruction atmosphere the point of the *Tefilah* is both to replace the daily sacrifice and to give hope of redemption and rebuilding of the Temple. Just as God had restored the Temple after the destruction of the First Temple, the people expected the same process after the Roman destruction of Jerusalem. Psalm 78, after recounting Israel's near total disobedience, ends with the messianic hope of the restoration of the Davidic dynasty that reigned during the First Temple:

> He did choose the tribe of Judah,
> Mount Zion, which He loved.
> He built His Sanctuary like the heavens,
> like the earth that He established forever.
> He chose David, His servant,
> and took him from the sheepfolds.
> He brought him from minding the nursing ewes
> to tend His people Jacob, Israel, His very own.
> He tended them with blameless heart;
> with skillful hands he led them.
>
> (PSALM 78:68–72)

Clearly all peoples can access God, and all will suffer from disobedience if they do not follow God's ways. It's not a matter of belief, but of action. Those who know the one God of the world will be blessed by acting correctly, and those who follow other gods and err in their ways will suffer.

What is our responsibility for the Jewish people? Melchizedek, the non-Jewish righteous king, blessed Abram for his actions. Psalm 78 praises those who act correctly and therefore preserve the covenant between God and Israel. How much do we consider the impact of our actions on the Jewish people and the world? The individual never gets mentioned here. All that matters is whether we act to benefit the Jewish people and God's world. The point is our relationship with God, as we are God's hands, arms, and feet in the world. But Israel could not live with fidelity toward God. If redemption depends on our ability to preserve God's covenant and act correctly, then God provides for us to live so as to bring ultimate satisfaction through moral conduct. Psalm 78 gives the account of Jewish history and our rebellions against living in harmony with God's wishes. While reciting the prayer, we ask ourselves where we would stand in the psalmist's critique.

Remarkably, Psalm 78 contains an entire biblical history of Israel and her rebellions. It seems Israel hasn't changed very much in three millennia. What a great reminder as we begin the *Tefilah* of where history can lead us and our responsibility to live in harmony with God's wishes for the world.

"Shield of Abraham": God's Promise

And what is God's role? The prayer closes stating that God is "Abraham's Protector [*magen*]." But what does that mean? Protector from or for what?

Genesis 15 opens with a vision to Abram:

> Fear not, Abram,
> **I am a shield [*magen*] to you;**
> Your reward shall be very great.

Abram despairs of ever having children and future descendants. But God promises that he will have a child who will inherit from him, that his descendants will be numberless, but that his people will be enslaved for four hundred years. Thus God will protect Abram, but life will not always be easy. That has been the history of our people for the last four thousand years, since Abram walked the earth. The prayer promises that God will protect Abram and his descendants.

When you think about it, does it not seem miraculous that the Bible would predict our survival for the last four thousand years and our connection to the Land of Israel and that has come to pass, even in our own generation? What predictions could you make for the year 6016 that you expect would really come true? If you are a Jew, your survival as part of a people, with God as your shield, part of a nation speaking the same language as Abram, half of whom are living in the same land as Abram and preserving the covenant established by Abram, is nothing less than miraculous, totally unexpected. Only one nation has survived without a homeland to sustain it. Something about God's people has enabled us to preserve and renew ourselves as a people that blesses the other nations over four millennia. And, if you are Jewish, you are part of that true miracle.

Does mere physical survival mean anything? I think not. If all time is the same, then the duration of the Jewish people means little to nothing. But if our endurance and the lessons we have taught humanity are a gift predicted four thousand years ago and that prediction has come true, how can we deny the ineffability of the result? No physical explanations can account for the fulfillment of the prophecy to be a blessing to the nations and survive where no other nation has. There are physical explanations for how this has come to be, so it is not a supernatural miracle. But the person who stands up and prays the same words that have passed the lips of Jews for two thousand years, connecting us to the lives of Abraham and Moses three thousand and four thousand years ago, experiences a sublime connection to history and a sense of immortality that is not expressible in mere words.

Perhaps this view of Jewish history is summarized in the other location that states that God is our protector, our shield:

> Adonai, my foes are so many!
> Many are those who attack me;
> many say of me,
> "There is no deliverance for him through God."
> **But You, Adonai, are a shield [*magen*] about me,**
> my glory, He who holds my head high.
>
> (PSALM 3:2–4)

For two-thirds of the time in which human beings have been conscious of our own unique place in the world and consciously recorded history, we Jews have been scribing our impressions of what it takes to survive and maintain our identity among the nations. That's a piece of the partnership that we've maintained with God. There must be a Powerful Force in the universe that enables us to sustain ourselves and be a blessing to humanity.

Gevurot: God's Power

Shcharansky Got It Right

You are forever mighty, Adonai: giving life to the dead, You are a mighty savior.

> [*From Shemini Atzeret to the first day of Passover, add:* You cause the wind to blow and You cause the rain to fall.]

> [*From the first day of Passover to Shemini Atzeret, add:* You bring down the dew.]

You sustain life with kindness, giving life to the dead with great mercy, supporting the fallen, healing the sick, and freeing the captive, and keeping faith with sleepers in the dust. Who is like You, Master of might, and who resembles You, a King who causes death and causes life, and causes salvation to flourish!

You faithfully give life to the dead. Blessed are You, Adonai, who gives life to the dead.[1]

In the ongoing American culture war over guns, both sides contend that their approach provides better protection. Perhaps we don't automatically think about it this way, but the key to safety is power. Power increases security. Indeed, much of the reason we accumulate power is to keep ourselves and those we love as safe as possible.

But is there such a thing as perfect safety?

Soviet refusenik Anatoly Shcharansky, now the renowned Israeli Natan Sharansky, was jailed by the Soviet Union in 1977 and released in 1986. Immediately after his release Shcharansky reported how, standing on the brink of freedom, he had refused to leave the Soviet Union. The Soviet authorities had confiscated the Hebrew book of Psalms whose inspiration had kept him going, a gift from his wife, Avital. Even after nine years of incarceration, seven of them in solitary confinement, Shcharansky refused to cross the bridge to freedom until the KGB returned the book. That book had given him strength![2]

How did Shcharansky risk torture and death, and thereby personally defeat the KGB and the Soviet Union? Simply put: his faith in God, in freedom, and in his supporters made him spiritually invincible even while physically vulnerable. The God of Israel standing by his side supplied the internal fortitude to withstand suffering. He could not prevent assaults; that was always in the hands of his captors. But with God's help, he could endure and triumph over whatever the Soviets threw his way.

What does it matter that God is mighty if we remain vulnerable?

"You Are Forever Mighty, Adonai": God's Power Protects Us

Our prayer opens with "You are forever mighty [*gibor*], Adonai," quoting Isaiah 42:13, "Adonai goes forth like a warrior [*gibor*]." It's a single-word quotation, but we have an excellent idea of the section of Isaiah the Rabbis desired we ruminate over while reading this prayer! How do we know? Because Isaiah 42:13 is from the haftarah, the prophetic reading, for the first Torah portion of the entire annual cycle, known as *Bereishit*.

What might be the lesson of that first Torah portion? As the most important Bible commentator, Rashi, famously wrote, the Torah has explained to us very clearly (Genesis 1:1), "What is the reason that the Torah commences with the account of the Creation?... All this earth belongs to the Holy One, blessed be He; He created it and will give it to whom He pleases."[3]

In other words, with this single-word quotation from the first haftarah of the entire year referring to the first Torah portion of the year, we
are being told, "God created and therefore owns everything." All history
lies in God's hands.

Power therefore becomes a synecdoche, a stand-in, for God: God is
power and protects God's people. If that's the case, we may ask, how did
we get into this lamentable situation of losing our land and the Temple
that connected us to God? Let's turn back to Isaiah.

As it happens, the Sephardi and Ashkenazi traditions choose
roughly the same verses in Isaiah for the haftarah, but the Sephardi
tradition restricts them. Here are the final verses of the Sephardi
version:

> Driven back and utterly shamed
> Shall be those who trust in an image,
> Those who say to idols,
> "You are our gods!"
>
> Listen, you who are deaf;
> You blind ones, look up and see!
> Who is so blind as My servant,
> So deaf as the messenger I send?
> Who is so blind as the chosen one,
> So blind as the servant of Adonai?
> Seeing many things, he gives no heed;
> With ears open, he hears nothing.
> Adonai desires His servant's vindication,
> That he may magnify and glorify His teaching.
>
> (ISAIAH 42:17–21)

God's servant is promised greatness, but having turned to idols requires
punishment. In the future God will vindicate him, but there will be travails until then.

The Ashkenazi haftarah continues further into the next chapter of
Isaiah, concluding with these words:

Fear not, for I am with you:
I will bring your folk from the East,
Will gather you out of the West;
I will say to the North, "Give back!"
And to the South, "Do not withhold!
Bring My sons from afar,
And My daughters from the end of the earth—
All who are linked to My name,
Whom I have created,
Formed, and made for My glory—
Setting free that people,
Blind though it has eyes
And deaf though it has ears."
All the nations assemble as one,
The peoples gather.
Who among them declared this,
Foretold to us the things that have happened?
Let them produce their witnesses and be vindicated,
That men, hearing them, may say, "It is true!"
My witnesses are *you*
—declares Adonai.
My servant, whom I have chosen.
To the end that you may take thought,
And believe in Me, and understand that I am He:
Before Me no god was formed,
and after Me none shall exist.

(Isaiah 43:5–10)

Here we witness Israel's first-century-CE condition foreshadowed in the sixth century BCE, seven hundred years earlier. The people presumed that the restoration following the destruction of the First Temple that resulted in the Second Temple would recur. In the previous prayer we saw a link to past generations and the heroes whose relationship with God continued after the second destruction. As God was their shield, so would God protect even after the Temple's downfall, because God owns the earth and all who live on it, distributing it as God sees fit.

But the problems they suffered characterize the human condition. As the Sephardi section of haftarah emphasizes, our ancestors worshiped idols. Our modern idols may not be constructed of biblical stone, but as we observed in the previous chapter, they enjoy the same function nonetheless. Each generation builds their own, and we live in the dispersion as they did. We are not only at a distance from God physically, but we have also been trained to keep ourselves at a distance from God spiritually. Hence we believe our idols are our only options. Discovering our way back becomes the first step into the modern spiritual challenge.

Reminding Us of Our Priorities

Years ago I wondered why idolatry is the most frequently mentioned sin in the Bible. But when I look around, I see that all of us create idols out of lesser things and serve them. Prophets like Isaiah preached to provide a corrective, a reminder that unless we prioritize serving the highest in every moment, we will fail ourselves and live in ways we will eventually regret. Isaiah's goal is to separate us from our baser selves. Reciting the *Gevurot* prayer specifically keeps this tendency before us three times daily and cautions us about its consequences. Attaching ourselves consistently to God keeps us spiritually safe and unafraid, as with Shcharansky. But it's tough work, requiring constant vigilance to prevent our seduction, particularly in our day of constant amusements. I am convinced that there is so much fear in the economically advanced world today, particularly in the United States, because we prefer our amusements and escapes to our values. We seem fearful of committing to a higher morality that will call us to account and we therefore prefer distractions from the serious business of living prophetically, like Isaiah or Shcharansky.

We call ourselves a religious nation, but we are constantly allowing ourselves to avoid responsibility and to stray to momentary satisfactions. We, as a nation, have been seduced. Isaiah recognized how tough it is to maintain our focus. Today, at this writing, there are handgun murders and fatal accidents in the newspapers daily, causing people to question their deepest commitments: how, precisely, do we choose life over death, for ourselves and others? Jewish literature, including our prayers, dedicates us to debating and choosing among values. It's yet to be determined which freedoms Americans prefer. Where do we attach our lives for the most rewarding spiritual commitment as opposed to momentary thrills?

One example: a woman went to her pediatrician's office with her young daughter. The doctor prescribed a brand-name medicine. With her smartphone in hand, the woman told the doctor she could not afford the price of the medication for her daughter. The doctor replied, "Yes, you can." After going back and forth several times, the woman asked, "Doctor, why are you insisting I can afford this medication?" His response? "Because you are carrying a smartphone whose monthly charge is more than the medication." The doctor was telling the woman to choose between her commitments: the medication for her daughter or the constant amusement of a smartphone.

Perhaps the lesson of Anatoly Shcharansky can be a guide for us. He lived an extreme reality, not some escapist Walter Mitty imagining his heroism, but a genuinely brave man negotiating his way in the realm of Realpolitik: the 1980s' Soviet gulag, with all its cruelties of beatings, hunger, and cold. Incarcerated and opposing the most powerful tyranny in the world at the time, he could not afford to rely on anything but truths. Putting his faith in God and trusting his intelligence, holding fast to the traditions of his people, he relied on God's power and controlled his personal destiny. He could not be tyrannized as long as he trusted in an all-powerful God.

Would God protect him from physical harm and keep him from pain? No, that's supernaturalism. He must have suffered terribly in isolation. But, with Shcharansky relying on the Eternal, the Soviets could not break his spirit, and so he won out, prevailing over those mightier physically but inferior spiritually.

Those who have the internal strength to rest on God's power can never be defeated.

Singing in the Rain

Inserted into the opening lines of this prayer about God's absolute power is acknowledgment of the need for rain and dew. In an agricultural society, success depends on seasonal moisture, as acknowledged in Job:

> **Does the rain have a father?**
> **Who begot the dewdrops?**
> From whose belly came forth the ice?
> Who gave birth to the frost of heaven?
> Water congeals like stone,
> And the surface of the deep compacts.
>
> (JOB 38:28–30)

God's point to Job is simply that God controls the physical laws of the world. The superb "out of the whirlwind" speeches in Job ascribe all power and understanding to God. We humans have to fit in to God's creation. As someone said regarding the 2015 California fires, "In a fight between nature and us, nature wins." The *Gevurot* insertion for half the year in Sephardi communities and the entire year in most Ashkenazi communities, "Who causes the rain to fall and the wind to blow," and its replacement, "Who causes the dew to fall," states the obvious in simple terms: Thank God for rain in its season. Without that we would not survive. Ultimately, we are not in control of our lives.

Consider that in the opening line of this prayer we proclaim God as "forever mighty," then give three examples: God gives life to the dead, provides salvation, and makes crops grow. In later blessings we will consider the meaning of salvation and see a petition for rain, not just thanking God for seasonal moisture. God gives life to the dead (think medicine), provides salvation (think spirituality that saves us from death while alive, like Shcharansky), and gives appropriate rain (think farmers and food). Now we will see that the source of these blessings is not only God's power, but also God's overwhelming love for God's people and God's holiness.

"You Sustain Life with Kindness": Negotiating the World Jewishly

Anthropologist Clifford Geertz taught that culture is to human beings what instinct is to animals. What, exactly, does that mean? A function of culture is to explain to us how we should behave.

The Jewish religion is a culture explaining to Jews the meaning and methods of living. So, for instance, the Torah tells us that we are created in God's own image and according to God's likeness. For thousands of years Jews have asked what, precisely, that means. Does God literally have eyes, ears, and a mouth? Well, no, although a biblical metaphor for anger is an inflamed nose! Instead, the Torah instructs, "You shall be holy, for I, Adonai your God, am holy" (Leviticus 19:2). The holiness we share with God is the meaning of being created in God's image. As God is holy, we have the capacity to be holy. But then, how do we implement that?

According to our tradition, to be created in God's image and to be holy define our best options for behavior. Holiness is not how we look or feel, it's what we do. First you "do" spiritual, then you "feel" spiritual. Not the reverse. Spirituality is not an emotion; it's a series of actions resulting in a method of living, an approach to life, a culture. Humans, and particularly Jews, can act morally. "As God buries the dead," tradition says, "so we bury the dead." "As God feeds the hungry, so we feed the hungry." This idea is termed *imitatio dei*; actively imitating God's holiness puts us in special relationship with God. To embody that capacity defines being created "in the divine image."

As Rabbi A. Lawrence Hoffman has taught us, prayer is acting out statements about who we intend to be, and then, rather than leaving those statements in the sanctuary when the prayers conclude, living by them even after leaving the sanctuary. Prayer becomes a sacred drama in which we cast ourselves, and rather than relinquish the character we portray after worship, we keep it going as long as possible upon reentering the world.

Our prayer about God's might now teaches us something about how we intend to sustain ourselves in the world, according to divine behaviors we duplicate in our own lives. It says that God "sustains life with kindness." The Hebrew word for "kindness" here is *chesed*, often translated "loving-kindness." It's a particular kind of selfless love, exemplified biblically by Ruth's love for her mother-in-law, Naomi, following the death of Naomi's husband and two sons, one of whom was Ruth's husband. But the word in our prayer comes from the repetition of *chesed* in Psalm 136, where it appears in every verse. The psalm lists many divine qualities: the God of goodness and steadfast love (verse 1), God the Creator (verses 6–9), who brought us out of Egypt (verses 10–24) and who feeds bread to all flesh (verse 25). But the upshot is that God's nature embodies selfless loving manifest to Israel and all flesh.

"Freeing the Captive and Keeping Faith with Sleepers in the Dust": Relying on God for Spiritual Safety

In Psalm 146 we find other moral qualities uncovered in our encounters with God, one of which we find quoted in our prayer (*matir asurim*, "freeing the captive"): "Adonai sets prisoners free" (*Adonai matir asurim*; Psalm 146:7). Shcharansky relied on this one, but the psalm lists others:

> Happy is he who has the God of Jacob for his help,
> whose hope is in Adonai his God,
> maker of heaven and earth,
> the sea and all that is in them,
> who keeps faith forever;
> who secures justice for those who are wronged,
> gives food to the hungry.
> **Adonai sets prisoners free;**
> Adonai restores sight to the blind;
> Adonai makes those who are bent stand straight;
> Adonai loves the righteous;
> Adonai watches over the stranger;
> He gives courage to the orphan and the widow.
>
> (Psalm 146:5–9)

So often in modern life we seek but do not find an absolute guidepost for our actions. How do we judge our own convictions and determine the path of our lives? The first part of this prayer by implication through the word "mighty" cautions us against our modern idolatries and forewarns of their consequences. Then the second part helps us guide our actions by selfless loving, *chesed*, and gives examples that holiness is determined by copying God's actions in dealing with humanity.

Humans use culture to guide us through the challenges of life, among them our fear at our vulnerabilities. Nothing can guarantee us absolute physical safety, but attachment to God can provide spiritual safety, resulting in an indomitable spirit, as exemplified by Anatoly Shcharansky's courage in the face of the Soviet regime.

Behind all of this fear is what Pulitzer Prize–winning psychologist Ernest Becker termed the denial of death, which is to say that death is humanity's greatest fear and vulnerability. All developed religions help humans cope with this foundational human angst. Five times in our prayer we emphasize that God delivers from death by resurrecting the dead. We never truly die.

Now before you roll your eyes or hopefully before you close the book, let me say that Judaism sees three types of resurrection in the world. The first is that nature dies in the autumn and is resurrected in the spring. We'd all agree on that one.

The second even my ultra-Orthodox friends laugh at. It's said that the soul leaves the body when we sleep and is returned to us when we awaken. That's the reason there's a prayer thanking God for the soul's return in the morning. One of my friends told me in yeshiva they'd laughingly debate if when they got up to pee in the middle of the night their souls returned, then left again when they went back to sleep.

The third resurrection we find in the second-century-BCE biblical book of Daniel:

> At that time the great prince, Michael, who stands beside the
> sons of your people, will appear. It will be a time of trouble, the
> like of which has never been since the nation came into being.
> At that time, your people will be rescued, all who are found

inscribed in the book. Many of those **that sleep in the dust** of the earth will awake, some to eternal life, other to reproaches, to everlasting abhorrence.

(Daniel 12:1–2)

Most modern, liberal Jews tell me that they know that Judaism does not believe in an afterlife. Of course, that's poppycock. Every Jewish movement for the last two millennia has affirmed an afterlife, including the most liberal. But, at least in my lifetime, it's rarely been discussed. Here Daniel, along with our prayer book, refers to "those who sleep in the dust" and their reawakening to immortal life.

Out of my personal experience from four decades in the rabbinate, I went from being a nonbeliever in afterlife to convinced of its existence. Personally, I believe that Catholic theologian Pierre Teilhard de Chardin was correct when he said, "We are not human beings having a spiritual experience; we are spiritual beings having a human experience." We intuit a sense of our eternality and that the struggles of this life are merely temporary, that there is something immortal about our existence.

Over the centuries Judaism has built up much speculation about this eternal existence. In the most general sense we postulate that the immortal part of each human, the soul, will go to an eternal home called *olam haba*, "the world to come," where it will reside until the coming of a messiah sent by God to rule the world. Then the nations will be united in peace, the messianic time, and the world will be ruled by God's chosen one from Jerusalem. The dead will be bodily resurrected, and souls united with bodies to live again.

Most liberal Jews do not believe in a messiah, but many do believe in *olam haba*, the world to come, the residence of the soul after the body's demise. Whereas the purpose of religion is to enable us to live a life of spiritual tranquility regardless of the threats we face over the course of a lifetime, many do find it easier to stare into the sun, as psychoanalyst Irving Yalom put it, with the assurance that death is merely a transition to a different, non-bodily existence.

Fear and safety are enormous modern concerns hanging over us like the sword of Damocles. But safety is achievable if we understand that we are safe in God's hands. God cannot protect our physical being, but we can triumph over our fears by choosing holiness as our way of life and God as our Protector. An enemy force, like the Soviet Union incarcerating Anatoly Shcharansky, or perhaps a disease attacking the body, may be able to control your physical existence, but it can never control your attitude and your mind. When we attach ourselves to God, painful things may occur to our bodies, but our minds and spirits can always remain free, and spiritually we will triumph.

Kedushah: Holiness

God Is Wholly Holy

> *Let us sanctify Your name on earth, as it is sanctified*
> *in the heavens on high, as written by Your prophet,*
> *"They called out one to another:*
> *'Holy, holy, holy is the Lord of hosts. The whole earth is*
> *full of His presence.'*
> *From across the way they offer blessing;*
> *'The presence of Adonai is blessed from His place.'"*
> *In Your holy scriptures it is written:*
> *"Adonai will reign forever, your God, Zion, for all*
> *generations. Hallelujah."*

For all generations we will tell of Your greatness and for all eternity proclaim Your holiness. Your praise, our God, will never depart our mouths, for You are a sovereign God, great and holy. Blessed are You, Adonai, the holy God.[1]

People desire to get close to God. If there's a power at the heart of the universe, there's a human attraction to connect with that power. That power we term "holiness," meaning both separate and powerful.

But how? What techniques will enable us to feel the pulsating Heart energizing existence, emanating from the core?

In the *Avot* prayer we saw the first method: identifying through our ancestors. Many years ago a woman told me tearfully and with some low-level anger veiled in her voice, like a cautious bear cub alone in the wilderness, how she really objected when the Reform movement changed to a new High Holy Day prayer book. "Every year," she said, "before the High Holy Days I go back to the bookshelf and retrieve my parents' prayer books. You've cut me off from those memories!" I wonder how many of us have had a similar experience. Continuity of liturgy connects us to family ties lost over the ages.

For this woman, ritual was among the last arteries connecting her to her beloved, although deceased, parents. The prayer book kept open the flow between them. Her origins were in her parents, and the High Holy Day memories strung together the high points of her life as though they all recurred simultaneously in her imagination. She connected through the prayer books and the God she first innocently experienced sitting beside them in holiday worship. The love she felt for her parents opened the access doors to God. The *Avot* prayer teaches us that as God related to the first generations of Jews—Abraham, Isaac, and Jacob; Sarah, Rebecca, Leah, and Rachel—so God remains connected to us, their spiritual and physical descendants.

The second prayer, *Gevurot*, describes God as the locus of power. God infuses creation with the life force, even reviving the dead. Whether it be the natural world with rain or sustaining human souls with *chesed*, divine loving-kindness, God empowers all living things. God also frees captives and provides for eternal life for those "who sleep in the dust." Therefore, benefiting from God's power and imitating God's ethical conduct, we come closer to God as protector and moral exemplar. When we duplicate God's acts in human form, we sympathetically draw closer to the Divine. A separation remains because we are not pretending to be God. But in acting godlike we increase the correspondence between God and ourselves.

Now, in the third prayer, the prayer of holiness, the *Kedushah*, we participate in the most intimate Divine-human encounter, the direct, mystical knowledge of God.

The *Kedushah* prayer appears in many forms in the prayer book. In the prayer after the *Barekhu* (the Call to Worship), the Creation prayer (*Yotzer*), it's called the *Kedushah d'Yotzer*. In the Torah service it's called the *Kedushah d'Sidra*. And as the third prayer in the *Tefilah*, the third of the standard three opening *Tefilah* prayers, it's called the *Kedushah d'Amidah*. There's the prayer read by the congregation, particularly in the evening service. Then there's the more elaborate prayers read by the prayer leader in the morning and afternoon services on weekdays and holidays. These last prayers, while each differs from the other, have the same intention and all contain the same three biblical quotations, to which we'll now turn.

Angels of God

If the biblical prophets listed their chapters chronologically, Isaiah 6 would be the first chapter in the most widely used prophetic book. It's Isaiah's call to prophecy in the year 742 BCE, "the year that King Uzziah died" (Isaiah 6:1). Isaiah portrays his personal vision visiting in God's royal court, witnessing the angelic seraphim surrounding God's glory and hearing their words of celestial praise. Directly before intense Presence, Isaiah stands overwhelmed, experiencing Absolute Being. He intuits himself to be ritually unclean, "of unclean lips" (Isaiah 6:5), unworthy of standing in proximity to ultimacy. A seraph cleanses his lips with a hot coal carried with tongs so that he may be purified to be sufficiently worthy and ritually pure. This is not simply Isaiah's selection as a prophet, but direct, personal knowledge of God, not by means of ancestors, not through imitating God's actions, not through cathecting to God's power in nature, but direct investment in God's personal presence, a disruption of earthly ties and removal to the realm of utter holiness.

Here's the timeless scene:

In the year that King Uzziah died, I beheld my Lord seated on a high and lofty throne; and the skirts of His robe filled the Temple. Seraphs stood in attendance on Him. Each of them had six wings: with two he covered his face, with two he covered his legs, and with two he would fly.

And one would call to the other,
"Holy, holy, holy
Is the Lord of hosts.
The whole earth is full of His presence."

The doorposts would shake at the sound of the one who called, and the House kept filling with smoke. I cried,

"Woe is me; I am lost!
For I am a man of unclean lips
And I live among a people
Of unclean lips;
Yet my own eyes have beheld
The King Lord of hosts."

Then one of the seraphs flew over to me with a live coal, which he had taken from the altar with a pair of tongs. He touched it to my lips and declared,

"Now that this has touched your lips,
Your guilt shall depart
And your sin be purged away."

Then I heard the voice of my Lord saying, "Whom shall I send? Who will go for us?" And I said, "Here I am; send me."

(Isaiah 6:1–8)

What do we have here? Literally, it's a fantastic scene within God's own court, modeled on the royal courts of the biblical world. The Divine Presence presides while sitting on a throne, with the entourage of angels constantly reciting God's praise with a specific litany reserved for the angelic retinue: "Holy, holy, holy ..."

Escaping Our Earthly Confines

Isaiah directly experiences standing in God's presence. Might we share that same immediate and personal knowledge?

This question has been posed by mystical seekers for millennia: How to encounter God directly? Perhaps if we, in a holy time of day, in a praying situation in which God is more accessible, sympathetically in touch with the heavenly court, recite the angelic words along with the seraphim, we can transport ourselves into the lofty realm and leave behind the earthly chains that bind us in both time and space.

In the prayer's choreography, many Jews will lift on the balls of their feet each time they say the word "holy," as if to draw nearer to the divine abode above. Jews who once claimed there was no mysticism in Judaism and totally rationalist Jews who have abandoned all thought of a direct spiritual experience are actually participating in the oldest liturgical piece of Jewish mysticism. But the passage does not end with the attempt at oneness with God, because the prophetic message continues.

When standing before absolute holiness we humans feel sinful and ritually unclean. Merely existing in such proximity to God evokes the "little lower than the angels" dilemma of human existence: we are material bodies aspiring to holiness. We seek greatness in partnership with God, but we fall short. How might we, at least momentarily, escape our earthly confines to abide with God? The closest we can come is to recite words spoken in God's presence as though we share the moment. This sympathy with God's closest, entirely spiritual beings perhaps can enable humans to shed our physical limitations and benefit from presence in the spiritual world.

The closest humans come to such bonding is the loss of self-consciousness in loving. When lovers melt emotionally into one another, blended as nearly a single creation, they approximate the mystical moment. The obvious difference is that love between two humans may be both physical and spiritual, whereas love of God is purely spiritual, uncomplicated by self-focused physicality. Yet, no doubt we understand why God's relationship to the People Israel is called a marriage by the kabbalists, given the similarities between the two relationships.

We have already learned that holiness, by definition, is participating in aspects of the Divine. Can the essence of Divine Being itself be shared, not just through action but also through proximity? Whether this is pure human imagination or an altered reality state, many believe this glimpse of Beingness is the closest we can come to the Godhead and a Reality above mere human understanding.

The Chariot of God

The second most famous mystical account in the Bible is found in the opening chapters of the prophet Ezekiel, the story of the chariot.

Ezekiel preached during the exile in Babylonia, often in symbols. The first two chapters of Ezekiel portray the vision of an extraterrestrial chariot. He says of his own experience by the river Chebar in Chaldea, "The heavens opened and I saw visions of God" (Ezekiel 1:1).

Ezekiel describes how the people of Israel will be brought back to life in their own land, but first he relates his personal encounter with God:

> He said to me, "O mortal, stand up on your feet that I may speak to you." As He spoke to me, a spirit entered into me and set me upon my feet; and I heard what was being spoken to me. He said to me, "O mortal, I am sending you to the people of Israel, that nation of rebels, who have rebelled against Me. They as well as their fathers have defied Me to this very day."
> (Ezekiel 2:1–3)

God has the prophet literally eat a scroll, presumably of God's teachings. Then Ezekiel says:

> Then He said to me: "Mortal, listen with your ears and receive into your mind all the words that I speak to you. Go to your people, the exile community, and speak to them. Say to them: Thus says the Lord God—whether they listen or not." Then a spirit carried me away, and behind me I heard a great roaring sound: **"The presence of Adonai is blessed from His place,"** with the sound of the wings of the creatures beating against one another, and the sound of the wheels beside them—a great roaring sound.
> (Ezekiel 3:10–12)

Ezekiel prophesies to the exiled community that has suffered the destruction of the First Temple. His words parallel the experience of the Jews in the late first century CE, also waiting hopefully to be redeemed from their exile. But, for the Jews of the first century, their exile was by Roman occupation of the Land of Israel.

Like Isaiah earlier, Ezekiel is visited by the physical and mystical Divine Presence commanding that he preach to a reluctant, recalcitrant, and rebellious Jewish people. Yet, God redeemed the people eventually, and the Rabbis of the post–Second Temple await a repeat redemption and return to previous glory, although their sins have condemned them to internal exile, their Temple utterly destroyed.

The quotation is enigmatic: "The presence of Adonai is blessed from His place." The Rabbis famously ask, "What is the place of God?" The answer comes from Psalm 24:1, "The earth is Adonai's and all that it holds."

Yet, consider what the question of God's place might have meant to those who suffered the loss of the Temple and prayed for its restoration in their own lives. The Temple, its Holy of Holies, and the Temple Mount had been "the place of God." Yet, Ezekiel seems to be reminding the people, along with the psalm, that God's presence not only fills the earth, but also that God can be encountered wherever God may be found by the individual. Thus, even while the stubborn and rebellious people are praying for a restoration of "God's place," they are reminded that God fills the earth and is not limited to a single place. This answer both fills the messianic expectation that feeds hope of the restoration of David's kingship and the coming of a messiah and also provides the comfort that God has not abandoned God's people, even in their present state of estrangement and internal exile.

Identifying the Chariot in Our Lives

Many people I know have had, like me, moments of experiencing God's presence "from His place," wherever that may be. Many of them quietly and without discussion, even avoiding disclosing to close friends, harbor happy, satisfying memories of personal revelation. Why don't they share such reminiscences?

Perhaps you have had a moment like this. I remember describing in a sermon my personal moment of revelation. Several people approached me after about their own experiences, including my own mother, who had never before shared with me that life memory! What is it about rationalists that we must exclude from our consideration real-life experiences that contradict the philosophical materialism we were taught in college and often at home? I have watched parents sit in congregations during their own child's bar or bat mitzvah, a dramatic moment filled with spiritual potential to which they have voluntarily brought their child, adamantly refusing to open a prayer book! Having entered their child into Jewish adulthood in the sanctuary and trained them to read from the Torah while leading prayers, they contradict and thereby negate the very sacred transition they insisted upon for their child! For a rabbi it's like watching a child washing with soap while playing in the mud—a totally wasted effort.

The Rabbis say that repenting while thinking of the next time you'll commit the same sin is like standing in a mikvah, a purifying bath, while holding a lizard, an animal that transmits ritual uncleanliness! Why do we insist on contradicting our own spiritual moments? Did both Isaiah and Ezekiel get it just right when God said to them:

Go, say to the people:

> "Hear, indeed, but do not understand;
> See, indeed, but do not grasp."

(Isaiah 6:9)

But the House of Israel will refuse to listen to you, for they refuse to listen to Me.

(Ezekiel 3:7)

What is there about us that we reject even our own experiences of God's presence and insist on explaining them in other than theological terms? I hear from people: "I was so moved at the baby naming, I cried." "You know, Rabbi, you moved me to tears in that eulogy." Are these merely shallow moments to be explained away as simple emotions, simple psychological variances on their otherwise banal day? Or are they, in fact, sacred incursions of holiness when we experience the divine chariot or see the courtyard of God in our own, contemporary terms?

Isaiah did not spend his entire life in the courtyard, and Ezekiel did not constantly view chariots. Famously, even Mother Teresa wrote that she had a single epiphanic moment that moved her to sacrificial human service for the rest of her life. Each of us accepts the same obligation: to identify the chariot in our lives. Perhaps one is enough for each of us. The question is not frequency; the question is identifying them as a message and making something of it.

Translating Encounter with Holiness into Action

Ezekiel accepted the communication and preached to his people about repentance and return. Isaiah took the encounter with God and spoke about justice accompanying ritual. In other words, the lesson is not merely a divine meeting, but how to both process and utilize that event as the basis for future action, as an orientation toward living. That's the lesson of the *Kedushah*, that the motivating encounter with holiness is available to us in life to experience God's presence and then to move forward heeding that awareness and motivated to act on it. The prophet does not simply encounter; he also translates that event into actions that move others to respond to God's presence within the Jewish people and humanity. Indeed, without both an authentic encounter and the message, he would not be a prophet.

Rabbi and theologian Abraham Joshua Heschel wrote:

> Prayer not verified by conduct is an act of desecration and blasphemy. Do not take a word of prayer in vain. Our deeds must not be a refutation of our prayers....
>
> Prayer is meaningless unless it is subversive, unless it seeks to overthrow and to ruin the pyramids of callousness, hatred, opportunism, falsehoods. The liturgical movement must become a revolutionary movement, seeking to overthrow the forces that continue to destroy the promise, the hope, the vision.[2]

Prayer, according to Heschel, is the ultimate human act of awareness of God and the universe, which must conclude with action, as the prophet's awareness of God's presence compels him to hear a divine message that he translates into action.

In the same fashion, our encounters with God can be made authentic and concretized in the real world not when we rationally analyze whether they historically occurred precisely as perceived, but when, like Isaiah, Ezekiel, and Heschel, we enable them to motivate our actions to inch the world toward God's ideals and actually feel the resultant exultation within ourselves. We make prayer real! When that moment of encounter with God at the baby naming increases your loving actions toward everyone in the room, even those with whom you might have been at odds; when your encounter with God on the street enables you to treat a stranger with kindness or "lift up the fallen," then you translate your chariot moment into redemption of God's world, a thought that we will deal with in the next chapter. Not even prophets lived exclusively within those divine moments of extraterrestrial perception. They were beginnings to understanding the reality of this spiritual/material world and how to operate in it, "What God requires of you," in the prophet Micah's words (Micah 6:8). They were infrequent epiphanies, a breakthrough from the divine into the mundane. The resultant consequences we build into our lives concretize those experiences and are the fruition of our prayers. When we emerge from worship prepared to make God real in the world, our encounters with God are actualized.

God Will Not Abandon Us

In the final biblical citation, we once again encounter Psalm 146, but not exactly as in the *Gevurot* prayer of our previous chapter. This time it's the final line of the psalm:

> Happy is he who has the God of Jacob for his help,
> whose hope is in Adonai his God,
> maker of heaven and earth,
> the sea and all that is in them;

who keeps faith forever;
who secures justice for those who are wronged,
gives food to the hungry.
Adonai sets prisoners free;
Adonai restores sight to the blind;
Adonai makes those who are bent stand straight;
Adonai loves the righteous;
Adonai watches over the stranger;
He gives courage to the orphan and widow,
but makes the path of the wicked tortuous.

Adonai will reign forever,
your God, Zion, for all generations.
Hallelujah.

The forever faithful God, who will not abandon us despite our fears resulting from the destruction of God's Temple, demands justice. The Talmud explains that the Jewish people morally transgressed. It was not the power of Rome but our lack of faithfulness to God's commandments that ultimately caused the destruction. That explains our failings and our loss of the Second Temple and political sovereignty. Nonetheless, this eternal God, who reveals through legislation and self-disclosure, will remain by our side as God's people in all of our travels, throughout our generations. Even as we catch glimpses of God's presence, we can also train ourselves to live by those revelations. Yet, despite our failures and unfaithfulness, God remains our companion, even in our times of despair and punishment. Ultimately, we will be redeemed.

The Thirteen
Weekday Blessings

Jerusalem, Here I Come

We have encountered God in three ways: ancestry (*Avot* prayer), power (*Gevurot* prayer), and holiness (*Kedushah* prayer). Now the *Tefilah* turns to its intended purpose. On weekdays we find at this point thirteen "intermediate benedictions." Intermediate between what? The opening three blessings, termed "Blessings of Praise," and the final three blessings, termed "Blessings of Thanks." How are these intermediates comparably described? On weekdays, but not on biblical holy days, we have thirteen "petitionary prayers."

The Talmud tells us two origins for these prayers: that they were written by the Men of the Great Assembly, the Sanhedrin, around 200 BCE; and that the chief rabbi, the *nasi*, at the end of the first century CE, Rabban Gamaliel II, commissioned one of the *Tana'im* (the plural of the term *Tana*, for the Rabbis of the first two centuries CE), Shimon haPakuli, to compose the *Tefilah*. But for what purpose?

The entirety of the *Tefilah* replaces the daily sacrifice, offered morning and afternoon, as we discussed previously. Words replace sacrifice! We have seen that there are three sections, each with a theme: praise, petition, and thanks. What about the nineteen individual benedictions? Does each have a theme of its own? We have studied

59

the first three prayers and seen each theme for ourselves. What about the next grouping, the intermediate thirteen recited on weekdays? Do they have a theme, and does that theme relate to Rabban Gamaliel's overall goal?

Yes, to both. According to a theory developed by Rabbi Leon Liebreich and taught by his student, Rabbi Lawrence A. Hoffman, PhD, the thirteen intermediate benedictions describe the process by which the messiah will come and restore the Davidic dynasty, returning Israel to its greatest national glory. What does that mean?

Jews believed God chose the Jewish people. In the biblical mind-set, that meant the Jewish nation was protected by God. The destruction of the Second Temple profoundly brought God's choice of Israel into question, forcing the people to come to grips with the meaning of their national existence in God's cosmology. To apply the same idea to the United States today, suppose the United States were massively defeated and occupied in war. That would cause people to deeply question American exceptionalism, and the people would demand answers. For the Jews of the first century CE, the answer became that God would send a king from the dynasty of the greatest biblical king, David, to reestablish the Davidic line and rebuild an independent Jewish state. The thirteen intermediate blessings describe the process of the coming of the messiah, step-by-step.

In the biblical world, Judea's kings were officially installed on the throne by anointing with oil. The Hebrew word for the one who is anointed is *mashi'ach*, which comes into English as a sound-alike word, "messiah." The role of the messiah is to bring political and spiritual redemption to the Jewish people and the world.

What Is Redemption?

Our thirteen prayers thus describe in detail the process of achieving redemption. What is redemption? Multiple biblical texts describe an era of peace and tranquility in which all the nations are ruled by a sovereign from Jerusalem. As the most basic definition, redemption is the reestablishment of the Davidic dynasty in Jerusalem and achieving the rule of

God with a descendant of King David on the Jerusalem throne. But in a larger sense, it's a time of wholeness and peace, a time of earthly perfection before the heavenly perfection yet to come. Before the rationalist modernity, and even to an extent today, that vision ran through Jewish thought consistently, among all movements and all thinkers, like a river nourishing the Garden of Eden.

The Hebrew word for "redemption" is *g'ulah*, and it's the theme of the prayer after the *Shema*, the prayer after a Torah reading, and one of the thirteen benedictions we are about to visit. It's the telos of Jewish history, the direction and destination of biblical and Rabbinic accounts of Jewish history and destiny.

But in a larger sense for us moderns, redemption is the ultimate completion of God's processes for our lives. If you believe that God has given you or the Jewish people a mission in life, the fulfillment of that mission personally or by the Jewish people is redemption. For instance, in the Reform Judaism of my childhood we did not believe in a messiah, but we substituted a "messianic age." That was not retirement at sixty-five, but an era of perfect peace, which we were attempting to achieve by campaigning for civil rights and opposing unjust wars, like Vietnam. We saw the process of history after World War II as leading to a world at peace, so horrible were the Nazi aggression and the atomic bomb that concluded the war, killing and maiming tens of thousands with a single explosion. Whereas Orthodox Jews believed God would send an individual as messiah to bring about the peaceful conclusion of history and God's rule on earth, we Reform Jews were taught to believe it was our religious occupation, in partnership with God, to save the world from injustice. We felt commanded to live as though we could, through our actions, create a world that would not need a messiah to achieve perfect harmony.

Da'at: Knowledge First

You favor people with knowledge and teach mortals understanding. Favor us with Your knowledge, understanding, and wisdom. Blessed are You, Adonai, who favors people with knowledge.[1]

Knowledge (*da'at*) and discernment are distinctly human qualities. The fact that we discern differences between things, that we possess the unique ability to interpret the events of our times, is a gift of God's love distinguishing humans from other animals, according to the famous genius Rabbi Moses Maimonides. In biblical Eden, at God's instruction, Adam distinguishes the names and functions of all animals. Adam and Eve consume the forbidden tree, ingesting the characteristics of the "tree of knowledge of good and evil," enabling humanity to discern between good and evil.

Among the biblical thirteen divine attributes listed in Exodus 34 is God's grace. God graciously bestows knowledge on humans, enabling humans to discern the meaning of events. This ability cuts both ways, as we are responsible to use this privilege to correctly interpret the events of our time and follow God's instructions to achieve divine goals for human history. The psalmist states:

> Take heed, you most brutish people;
> fools, when will you get wisdom?
> Shall He who implants the ear not hear,
> He who forms the eye not see?
> Shall He who disciplines nations not punish,
> **He who instructs men in knowledge (*da'at*)?**
> Adonai knows the designs of men to be futile.
>
> (PSALM 94:8–11)

The first assertion in the petitions establishes our human ability to get it right, to see clearly what is happening and work toward God's goals for the Divine-human partnership. Amazingly, the greatest problems society suffers from today are rooted in the use of discernment for our personal advantage exclusively, not considering the Divine-human partnership. "What's best for society?" is often not what we hear people ask when they consider energy consumption or personal comfort issues, like heating and cooling our homes or driving our cars.

In the aftermath of the Roman cataclysm and through the Middle Ages, how could the Jewish people correctly discern the meaning of these events? The conclusion: God gave us the ability to see and gain knowledge, correctly interpreting God's will and determining our reaction. Would that we'd do the same in our own life crises and for our national purpose as our culture wars in 2016 threaten our very lives.

How complex might this process have been in the first century of the Common Era? We possess 20/20 eyesight when looking back twenty centuries, but they did not have the advantage of seeing the trajectory of history over time the way we do now. How did they get it right?

Consider the thought experiment of living in similar times to theirs. Perhaps that will shed some light on how difficult their situation was in context. Just sixty-eight years ago Jews established the first Jewish commonwealth in two thousand years. What does this mean? Is this the beginning of our redemption, as the Israeli Chief Rabbinate claims in a nearly universally read Jewish prayer? After the Six-Day War in 1967, just twenty-two years after the decimation of the Jewish people in the Holocaust, Jews felt what many believed to be the hand of God in Israel's triumph. The Jewish world expressed so much pride at the victory that it is not an exaggeration to say those six days changed Jewish destiny worldwide. It invigorated the Soviet Jewry movement within the former Soviet Union. It changed what the college-age Jewish generation demanded from the established, national American Jewish community, as expressed at the national meeting of Jewish Federations in 1969. Israel became such a popular college destination that two years after the 1967 war the American study abroad program at Hebrew University had tripled in size, necessitating building new dorms and programs. Many Jews who had been universalists in practice and ethics became universalists in ethics but particularists in practice, turning away from interfaith relations to developing personal, new adaptations of historical Jewish practices like wearing *kippot* and keeping kosher. All of this resulted as the aftershock of a nearly apocalyptic war lasting less than a week. Of course, the impact of those six days has complicated Middle Eastern politics ever since.

Evangelical Christians interpret Israel's 1948 founding as a precursor to the return of their messiah and the eschaton, with a final rapture for believers, Armageddon, and the triumph of God. Liberal Jews interpret the same events as establishing a Jewish homeland to save Jews from persecution, consistent with the plan laid out by Theodor Herzl when he founded the Zionist movement. Discernment of divine intention is a very challenging skill, and each grouping is often fervently convinced of the correctness of their interpretation of events. What did the founding of Israel and the Six-Day War nineteen years later mean? That's still being determined, with different religious groups living out their sectarian interpretations in their own lives.

Using Our God-Given Ability to Discern Truth

Now perhaps we can comprehend the stakes of composing and disseminating these thirteen blessings. The impact of the Rabbis' interpretation of history lay on the line, and the message has overshadowed the Jewish understanding of historical events ever since. Similarly, in our own day we are challenged to determine whether God's plan is reflected in the events many living Jews remember personally. The God-given ability to discern is indeed critical to our lives.

The prayer asks God to "favor us with your knowledge, understanding, and wisdom." Jeremiah instructs:

> "Turn back, rebellious children," declares Adonai. "Though I have rejected you, I will take you, one from a town and two from a clan, and bring you to Zion. And I will give you shepherds after My own heart, who will pasture you with **knowledge and wisdom**.
>
> "And when you increase and are fertile in the Land, in those days," declares Adonai, "men shall no longer speak of the Ark of the Covenant of Adonai, nor shall it come to mind. They shall not mention it, or miss it or make another. At that time, they shall call Jerusalem 'Throne of Adonai,' and all nations shall assemble there, in the name of Adonai, at Jerusalem. They shall no longer follow the willfulness of their evil hearts. In those days, the House of Judah shall go with the House of Israel; they shall come together from the land of the north to the Land I gave your fathers as a possession."
>
> (Jeremiah 3:14–18)

Although the prophet Jeremiah lived at the end of the seventh century BCE and spoke of events in the First Temple, these verses seem addressed to the Jews of the first century CE as well. God will grant knowledge and wisdom, which will be followed by reunification of the people in Jerusalem. The evil that brought God's punishment will be reversed, and Israel will be reestablished in the Land.

These verses can be read the same way today. The biblical kingdoms of Israel (today called Samaria) and Judea will be reunited. These verses can be read as giving great comfort to modern Israelis regarding their own political situation and God's will of ingathering the exiles to a modern Jewish state. It envisions a time of peace, with Israel at the center of the world.

In a larger view, the ability to discern has established the Jewish people's great success worldwide. Jewish scientists have changed the world, and Israel today is the most entrepreneurial of nations. The ability to discern truth is foundational for Jews everywhere, and certainly the basis of all Jewish tradition. The Talmud, the basic Jewish text, constantly debates how Jews should behave in every aspect of life. Studying the Talmud requires great discernment of the interpretation of the texts the Rabbis used. If there is a single quality on which Jewish life depends, it's discernment.

Teshuvah: Repentance—Not for Yom Kippur Only

Bring us back to Your Torah, our Father, draw us near to Your service, our King, and turn us back, in perfect repentance before You. Blessed are You, Adonai, who takes pleasure in repentance.[2]

After acknowledging God's gift of knowledge and discernment, what's the next step? It's repentance (*teshuvah*). There are no lengthy biblical quotations in this prayer, but fourteenth-century Seville rabbi David Abudraham connects the first of the three parts of the prayer with the famous prayer in Nehemiah 9:34, which we have seen before:

> And now, our God, great, mighty, and awesome God, who stays
> faithful to His covenant, do not treat lightly all the suffering

that has overtaken us ... from the time of the Assyrian kings to
this day. Surely You are in the right with respect to all that has
come upon us, for You have acted faithfully, and we have been
wicked. **Our kings, officers, priests, and fathers did not follow Your Teaching, and did not listen to Your commandments or to the warnings that You gave them.** When they
had their own kings and enjoyed the good that You lavished
upon them, and the broad and rich land that You put at their
disposal, they would not serve You, and did not turn from their
wicked deeds. Today we are slaves, and the Land that You gave
our fathers to enjoy its fruit and bounty—here we are slaves on
it! On account of our sins it yields its abundant crops to kings
whom You have set over us. They rule over our bodies and our
beasts as they please, and we are in great distress.

(Nehemiah 9:32–37)

Returning to Torah after straying into quotidian interests reminds
Abudraham of the story of a king's son who was captured at a young
age by a foreign people and later requested to return home. He's not
ashamed by the request because he says, "I am returning to my inheritance." To ignore Torah study simply to engage in trivialities is likened
to being captured by foreigners, because Jews' estrangement from Torah
is opting for residence in a foreign land, disconnection from our true
selves. Choosing Torah is returning home, even if we've never been
there before.

A similar story appears in the Christian Bible's book of Luke: the
parable of the prodigal son. While the stories differ significantly in
details, both testify to God's desire to welcome home God's child no
matter where he has strayed.

"Bring Us Back to Your Torah": Coming Home to Jewish Spirituality

The story typifies the majority of our contemporary Diaspora Jewry
who, while living Jewish lives, are often woefully ignorant of Torah and
Jewish learning. If you have chosen to read this book and have gotten

this far, you may well be among those who have selected their heritage after straying for "trivialities." If so, you can judge for yourself whether the drive for a spiritual life is fulfilled by a return to Torah, with "Torah" encompassing all Jewish texts. Often Diaspora Jews have never been exposed to the depths of Jewish spirituality and when they discover it are both surprised and delighted by its potential for instilling the feeling of "coming home" for the first time.

This return occurs in an age too often devoid of spiritual satisfaction. Any culture orbits around foundational values acknowledged by the majority of its members. But we live in a time and place where no set of values is universally acknowledged. Even worse, most people do not possess a personal set of mores they find ultimately satisfying. We are like shallow-rooted trees in a storm. Not to murder or steal is not up for debate theoretically. But even the meaning of "murder" and "theft" cannot be agreed upon. Is abortion murder? When does a fetus become a person? Does cheating on taxes or taking from Walmart constitute theft? Is it smarter or more realistic to just "get away with" whatever you can and pay the consequences if caught? Does karma actually work and will the universe call us to account for our transgressions?

These real cultural debates point to a deficient spiritual core, unable to nourish the body politic, which can be reinvigorated by a return to Torah learning and the Torah-values debates accumulated over centuries. Even if we choose to disagree with the Rabbis' conclusions, we have discovered a principled basis of thought to guide our deliberations for the shared values on which to base both a society and our individual identity.

For instance, historical Jewish texts do not agree with the conclusions of the worldwide debate over gay and lesbian rights. But the very fact that we Jews have a trackable debate, elucidating values to be reconsidered in every age, which then spawned a reconsideration of those values and the adoption of new principles for practice by Judaism's liberal streams, testifies to the value of historical spiritual discussions. Instead of strictly following the precedent delineated by Leviticus 18:22, "Do not lie with a male as one lies with a woman," modern streams have substituted the ideal that all people are created in the divine image, "Let us make man in our image, after our likeness" (Genesis 1:26). Judaism over more than two millennia refined a clear method of both debating spiritual issues and altering principles when demanded by the times. Torah debates identify the subjects and the principles involved in arriving at spiritually satisfying conclusions.

The very idea that we are describing here, that there is a process leading to something called "redemption," an ultimate meaning to life, stimulates the debate absent in most people's lives and yet necessary to human fulfillment. Our psyches demand that each person personally settle the ultimate spiritual question of redemption: what purpose does my life serve in the world?

"Draw Us Near to Your Service": Equating Prayer and Sacrifice

Every literate Jew of the first century CE would know the famous quotation from the prophet Hosea, "Return [*shuvah*], O Israel, to Adonai your God" (Hosea 14:2). It lends its name to the Sabbath between the High Holy Days, Rosh Hashanah and Yom Kippur, called Shabbat Shuvah, "the Sabbath of Return," when we read Hosea 14:2–10, which concludes:

> He who is wise will consider these words,
> He who is prudent will take note of them.
> For the paths of Adonai are smooth;
> The righteous can walk on them,
> While sinners stumble on them.
>
> (HOSEA 14:10)

The cataclysm called the *Churban HaBayit*, the Destruction of the Temple, occurred, according to Rabbinic assessment, because God punished Israel for her sins, the "stumbling of sinners." When the nation sins, it disrupts the natural cosmic flow and causes chaos that destroys the divinely created stability. Repentance and forgiveness accomplished through sacrifices or prayer reverse that process of social disintegration and restore the cosmic order. The Rabbis, while necessarily instituting the new system of Torah interpretation to replace the destroyed sacrificial system, nonetheless believed in the return of the sacrificial cult as part of the coming of the messianic times.

Therefore the first of the three parts of this prayer emphasizes return to Torah, but the second and parallel phrase, "draw us near to Your service," speaks of *avodah*, the Hebrew word for "service" ambiguously referring to both sacrifice and worship.

The second paragraph of the *Shema* prayer includes the instruction "to love Adonai your God and **to serve Him with all your heart**." The Rabbis tellingly comment, "What is to serve Him with all your heart? It is prayer!" (Babylonian Talmud, *Taanit* 2a). By using the Hebrew word *avodah*, the verse connects prayer with the sacrificial system, equating the two. The loss of the sacrificial system did not destroy access to God and repentance. The Rabbis substituted prayer for sacrifice, and the way was smoothed by the conflation of both concepts into a single word.

"Turn Us Back, in Perfect Repentance before You": Renewal through Repentance

The prayer proceeds to the third request, reminiscent of the very end of the biblical book of Lamentations, which bewails the first destruction in the sixth century BCE:

> **Take us back, Adonai, to Yourself**,
> And let us come back;
> Renew our days as of old!
>
> (LAMENTATIONS 5:21)

The words are not exactly the same, and therefore it is not a quotation. But the sentiment is clear. The prayer says, "Turn us back, in perfect repentance," while Lamentations entreats, "Take us back," which, through a pun in the Hebrew, could be translated either as "Cause us to return" or "Cause us to repent." The reference and sentiment are more apparent in the Hebrew than the English translation. God's call to repentance after destruction, however, is eminently clear in both.

Selichah: After Repentance, Forgiveness

Forgive us, our Father, for we have sinned. Pardon us, our King, for we have transgressed, for You forgive and pardon. Blessed are You, Adonai, who is gracious and quick to forgive.[3]

While the Bible is chock full of divine anthropomorphisms, our rabbis are much more comfortable describing God's actions than attempting to attribute physical qualities to God.

The most renowned set of divine qualities, the thirteen attributes, appears in Exodus 34:5–7:

> Adonai came down in a cloud; He stood with [Moses] there, and proclaimed the name Adonai. Adonai passed before him and proclaimed: "Adonai! Adonai! a God compassionate and gracious, slow to anger, abounding in kindness and faithfulness, extending kindness to the thousandth generation, forgiving iniquity, transgression, and sin; yet He does not remit all punishment, but visits the iniquity of parents upon children and children's children, upon the third and fourth generations."

By Torah's own direct description, sin forgiveness (*selichah*) is part of God's essence, which our prayers of repentance fit into like a hand into a glove. Multiple examples appear in the Bible. For instance, when Israel refuses to enter the Promised Land, God condemns them to forty years in the wilderness, until the slave generation dies out (Numbers 14). God does not disown or kill them where they stand in recompense for their rebellion, as God does with the rebels in the aftermath of Korach's rebellion (Numbers 16). The rebels against entering the Promised Land repent their ways; Korach's rebels challenging Moses's right to leadership do not. In the rebellion against entering the Land, God simply delays God's timeline and alters course, realizing that the slaves would never liberate themselves into self-directing people. They'd always be afraid. Apparently there's a limit to God's control of human actions, but also there's a difference in types of rebellion, dependent upon repentance!

"Forgive Us": It's Up to Us

Since we know that it is God's nature to forgive, after we repent we might expect God's forgiveness. But we must request! Forgiveness does not just occur automatically, dragged in the wake of repentance. We all know this from our own lives. After you say, "I'm sorry," you say, "Will you forgive me?"

All sins, whether against God directly or against another person, contain an element of rebellion against God's rules. Once we have asked forgiveness of another person and repented our sin by confessing the sin and intending never to repeat it, we can in good conscience turn to God and ask for what is in God's nature to grant. But confessing to another person and then asking for forgiveness requires humility, and that's difficult for many of us to achieve. It's one thing to admit to ourselves and even to God in private that we have strayed. But then becoming vulnerable to another person's judgment of us and demonstrating that we are lower in status because we are asking to be forgiven, that's excessive for some people. Too much humbling! The irony is that confession and forgiveness are the front door into a spiritual life.

Embedded here we find an essential attribute of the Jewish view of divine cosmology: how the world works. God designed the world as a finely greased machine with infinite gears. Sin tosses grit into the works and mucks up the interactions. It unbalances the natural orderly flow of the world. Repentance and forgiveness clean up the parts and return them to their default settings, restoring harmony. In this sense, our repentance and forgiveness not only resolve relational conflicts but also possess cosmic implications beyond the immediate parties to the dispute. We are, so to speak, retooling the gears of God's technology so that the machine will work most efficiently and with the least pain and suffering. Spirituality enables us to experience the inside workings of the machine, but humility is the entrance ticket.

God's forgiveness appears repeatedly in the Torah and Prophets. Perhaps the most famous we find in a haftarah used for public fast days:

> Seek Adonai while He can be found,
> Call to Him while He is near.

> Let the wicked give up his ways,
> The sinful man his plans;
> **Let him turn back to Adonai,**
> **And He will pardon him;**
> To our God,
> For He freely forgives.
> For My plans are not your plans,
> Nor are My ways your ways
> —declares Adonai.
>
> (ISAIAH 55:6–8)

This chapter of Isaiah concludes seven chapters about the reconciliation and restoration of Israel to God during the first exile after the destruction of the First Temple. The events exactly parallel the emotional and theological status of the Jewish people at the turn of the first century CE and the hope embodied by these thirteen benedictions for the messianic redemption. Clearly fulfillment of their fondest hope requires repentance and forgiveness, as it had six centuries earlier as recorded by God's prophet Isaiah. God will again restore a repentant Israel because it is God's nature to forgive!

G'ulah: Redemption—The Ongoing Redeemer

See our affliction, and fight our fight, redeem us quickly for the sake of Your name, for You are a mighty redeemer. Blessed are You, Adonai, who redeems Israel.[4]

We've established the requirements to restore God's world: knowledge with discernment, repentance, and forgiveness. Being restored to God, we are ready to set the messianic process in motion. We therefore request redemption. But based on what? How do we know that God will redeem?

We have already alluded to historical precedent with the destruction of the First Temple and return from exile, followed by rebuilding the destroyed Temple in the sixth century BCE. The prophet Jeremiah, who prophesied about the coming destruction resulting from Israel's sins (and must have been a rather dour fellow for all of his negativity), is the perfect person to tell us that with all of the things Israel has done wrong, they nonetheless can be restored:

> Thus said the Lord of hosts:
> The people of Israel are oppressed,
> And so too the people of Judah;
> All their captors held them,
> They refused to let them go.
> **Their Redeemer is mighty,**
> **His name is Lord of hosts.**
> He will champion their cause—
> So as to give rest to the earth,
> And unrest to the inhabitants of Babylon.
> A sword against the Chaldeans
> —declares Adonai.
>
> (JEREMIAH 50:33–35)

Much of the book of Jeremiah is given to berating Israel for her sins. As the book comes to its conclusion, we turn to condemnations of the surrounding nations and a promise of redemption for Israel, with God's help. How perfect! Even though Jeremiah roundly condemned Israel's actions and famously promised destruction, he never gives up on God's resurrecting the people in their land. It's as if your terribly severe father, who berated you for every mistake, suddenly turned around and said, "But you know what? You're doing the right thing here, and it's going to turn out okay." What a surprise and relief! You heave a sigh.

Both Jeremiah's quotation and the sentiment are perfect for the location in the *Tefilah*. Having just completed repentance and forgiveness, as Jeremiah would have wanted, we turn to his promise that God has not forsaken us. Just as God restored God's people to the Land of Israel after the first cataclysm at the hands of the Babylonians, the same ought to recur after the Roman destruction or in the succeeding centuries. Destruction and restoration are inherent to the process of sin and redemption, just as occurred with your parents when you rebelled and were punished but they loved you anyway, and eventually the family came back together.

The actual prayer language, however, occurs in Psalm 119:

> See my affliction and rescue me,
> for I have not neglected Your teaching.
> **Champion my cause and redeem me**;
> preserve me according to your promise.
> Deliverance is far from the wicked,
> for they have not turned to Your laws.
> Your mercies are great, Adonai;
> as is Your rule, preserve me.
> Many are my persecutors and foes;
> I have not swerved from Your decrees.
> I have seen traitors and loathed them,
> because they did not keep Your word in mind.
> See that I have loved Your precepts;
> Adonai, preserve me as befits Your steadfast love.
> Truth is the essence of Your word;
> Your just rules are eternal.
>
> (PSALM 119:153–160)

While Psalm 119 is written in the first person singular, the prayer alters the language to first person plural, because we pray in community for the entire House of Israel.

Psalm 119 is an alphabetical acrostic, with an entire stanza devoted to each letter. This is the *reish* stanza, the "R" of the Hebrew alphabet. Its thoughts hold together both physically and thematically.

We now know, from neurobiological research, that there are moral categories embedded in the human brain. Theoretically these developed as part of Darwinian evolution. Among these are the polarity of fairness/cheating, around which all cultures develop specific rules. Here the psalmist, in hoping for God's redemption, speaks of his loathing for those who are traitors to God and points out that the supplicant is on God's side and opposes the wicked. He presupposes that God favors justice and that there will be divine reward for the righteous.

Thus, the psalm links an innate moral category that causes immense human frustration to God's redemption, the problem of good and evil. We have been punished because we deserved it, having rebelled against God's laws. But this rebellion is not simply ritual in nature. It involves morality as well, and God sides with the righteous against the wicked. But as Jeremiah points out in the previous quotation, the nations surrounding Israel have not been better, and God will punish them. We pray for God to appreciate Israel's moral qualities and, now that we have been punished for our sins, to redeem us and return us to political independence.

Our Eternal Covenant with God

The prayer raises the issue of why we might deserve God's attention and favor. The entire Bible assumes the relationship with God established with Abraham and Sarah and their descendants in Genesis 17. This eternal covenant cannot be destroyed and has implications for all humanity. Many people today look at world events, particularly in the Middle East, and interpret them in light of their assumptions about this covenant between the Jewish people and God.

Isaiah 47 speaks of Israel's sins against God by turning away and seeking their security through other means. Israel put their faith in other methods, like sorcery and astrology, and the result was disastrous. But in the first five verses of the chapter we see that the true God of Israel, with whom Abraham established a covenant long before, actively continues to abide by that agreement, while punishing those nations that were the instruments of God's punishment for Israel.

> Get down, sit in the dust,
> Fair Maiden Babylon;
> Sit, dethroned, on the ground,
> O Fair Chaldea;
> Nevermore shall they call you

The tender and dainty one.
Grasp the handmill and grind meal.
Remove your veil,
Strip off your train, bare your leg,
Wade through the rivers.
Your nakedness shall be uncovered,
And your shame shall be exposed.
I will take vengeance,
And let no man intercede.
Our Redeemer—Lord of hosts is His name—
Is the Holy One of Israel.
Sit silent; retire into darkness,
O Fair Chaldea;
Nevermore shall they call you
Mistress of Kingdoms.

(ISAIAH 47:1–5)

Just as God's nature is to forgive, God's nature is to redeem. It's not that God once redeemed Israel from Egypt, but that God is the ongoing Redeemer. That's God's character when circumstances are correct.

Refu'ah: First God Heals

Heal us, Adonai, that we shall be healed. Save us that we shall be saved, for You are our praise. Bring complete healing to all our wounds.

For You are our sovereign, steadfast, merciful healing God. Praised are You, Adonai, who heals the sick among His People Israel.[5]

Did you have a relative who said, when you got the sniffles, "What did you do wrong?" I have friends who did. It freaked them out and made them believe that bad conduct resulted in sickness, like a negative Santa Claus that punished rather than rewarded. Today most of us believe that the content of our character is a separate issue from the functioning of our bodies. Before modern medicine, and certainly in biblical and

Rabbinic times, our ancestors believed that illness results from sin as pain results from a fist fight.

More important, the prospect of illness often terrifies us, particularly painful or life-threatening illness. We'd do almost anything to avoid suffering, and many will turn to whatever methods are offered to ward off or cure both anguish and death.

The prophet Jeremiah made clear that torment operates as part of God's larger plan:

> Assuredly,
> All who wanted to devour you shall be devoured,
> And every one of your foes shall go into captivity;
> Those who despoiled you shall be despoiled,
> And all who pillaged you I will give up to pillage.
> **But I will bring healing to you**
> **And cure you of your wounds.**
>   (JEREMIAH 30:16–17)

Have you ever been really ill, so ill that your body's capacity to heal seemed like a gift of God's creation? For me it's a marvel that the body possesses the capacity to rebound. In 2010 my back failed so badly that I could do nothing but lie flat without excruciating, mind-coagulating pain. After having four vertebrae fused and undergoing ten weeks of recovery, I was astonishingly pain free! No one predicted the positive outcome, even the surgeon. But it happened. The connection between the two, illness and then health, is awesome. Let's remember Jeremiah's biblical perspective as expressed in Deuteronomy:

> If you fail to observe faithfully all of the terms of this Teaching [*Torah*] that are written in this book, to reverence this honored and awesome Name, Adonai your God, Adonai will inflict extraordinary plagues upon you and your offspring, strange and lasting plagues, malignant and chronic diseases. He will bring back upon you all the sicknesses of Egypt that you dreaded so, and they shall cling to you. Moreover, Adonai will bring upon

you all the other diseases and plagues that are not mentioned in this book of Teaching [*Torah*], until you are wiped out. You shall be left a scant few, after having been as numerous as the stars in the skies, because you did not heed the command of Adonai your God. And as Adonai once delighted in making you prosperous and many, so will Adonai now delight in causing you to perish and in wiping you out; you shall be torn from the Land that you are about to enter and possess.

(Deuteronomy 28:58–63)

In other words, sin results in illness and indicates a reversal of the beneficence promised in Genesis 17, when God established a covenant with Abraham, promising the Land. It's a benchmark, so to speak.

Strangely, even in this seemingly superstition-rejecting and rationalist age, many people, when threatened with illness, revert to the same insecurity and ask, "How did I bring this upon myself? What was my sin?" The search for answers as to the reason for affliction and death is as poignant in contemporary lives as ever. Even with better medicine, perhaps particularly with better medicine, we have trouble distinguishing an ultimate reason or purpose for human suffering. Often people pray specifically because they believe it will help heal themselves or those they care about and love.

The idea that prayer aids in health is promoted in the book of Numbers, with the shortest prayer in the Bible, six Hebrew words, two of which are "please [*na*]."

God, please, heal, please, her [*El na r'fa na lah*].

(Numbers 12:13)

This prayer is offered by Moses to God when Miriam, Moses's sister, is punished by God with a skin disease for slandering Moses. Sin leads to illness, just as repentance leads to divine forgiveness, and ultimately to healing.

Jeremiah provides our prayer's words for the urgent request directed to God:

Heal me, Adonai, and let me be healed;
Save me, and let me be saved;
For You are my praise.

(JEREMIAH 17:14)

Here, as previously, our prayer takes the biblical first person singular and converts it grammatically into a first-person plural group prayer.

Reclaiming the Personal Prayer

Jewish prayers historically were replete with personal petitions for health, along with prayers for the health of friends and other loved ones. Health questions go to our deepest human insecurities, causing us, sometimes literally, to stand horrifyingly naked and vulnerable before ourselves and the world. Classical Reform Judaism removed healing prayers as being too nonrational. They struck earlier generations as asking God to supernaturally intervene, contrary to common sense and natural law. The liberal Judaism of the 1950s and '60s focused more on social justice than on personal connection to God.

But composer/song leader/liturgist Debbie Friedman (*z"l*) introduced a radical new spiritual element into liberal streams of Judaism when she composed her *Mi Shebeirach* prayer in the 1990s. Its words and melody transformed Reform Judaism and renewed an intimate part of our liturgy that had been removed with the healing prayer.

Mi Shebeirach

Mi shebeirach avoteinu
   M'kor hab'rachah l'imoteinu
   May the source of strength,
   Who blessed the ones before us,
   Help us find the courage to make our lives a
   blessing,
   and let us say, Amen.
Mi shebeirach imoteinu
   M'kor hab'rachah l'avoteinu

Bless those in need of healing with *r'fuah sh'leimah*,
The renewal of body, the renewal of spirit,
And let us say, Amen.

(DEBBIE FRIEDMAN)

Until recent times, in the midst of the blessing for healing the praying person had the option to personalize the petition:

May it find favor before You, my God and my ancestors' God, that You speedily send complete healing from the heavens, spiritual healing and physical healing to [insert name here] who is sick, along with others who are sick among Israel.[6]

So often modern Jews feel removed from prayer's immediacy, from prayer as a personal response to their existential condition, like sickness. Prayer can't be a relevant force in people's lives if we can't expose our deepest desires. Judaism teaches, "The Merciful One desires the heart" (Babylonia Talmud, *Sanhedrin* 106b; Zohar, Raya Mehemna to *Parashat Kee Tetzei*, p. 281b). When I ask Reform Jews, "Do you pray frequently?" most answer "yes." But they don't pray formulary, organized prayers, as from a book. Rather, many stop at least once a day to make a request of God or offer thanks informally, without resorting to a formal prayer structure. But Debbie Friedman's *Mi Shebeirach* and the many compositions that followed from other composers brought home the immediacy of petition in community.

What touches us more deeply than debilitating illness? When Job suffers three calamities and loses all that is dear to him, the tragedies occur in escalating order of severity to him personally: first he loses his wealth, then his children, and finally his personal health, and he is left sitting miserably on a dung heap, scratching his sores. Whether we pray for a miraculous intervention to cure us or for a natural healing, or whether we simply pray for the ability to endure the illness with grace and dignity, the traditional fourth of the thirteen weekday blessings resonates within us as a real nexus between our day-to-day mundane concerns and God's existence. Indeed, I know people who attend worship solely for the purpose of praying to benefit someone who is sick.

Not all of this need be an attempt to achieve miracles. Some pray for the capacity to bear creatively with illness rather than for a cure of a permanent disease. There is also today considerable literature around the healing nature of prayer within a religious community. When I was a child, people didn't offer such private prayers because they seemed superstitious, although we craved the embracing healing of God's presence in our troubles. People were, and surveys tell us often are, ashamed of illness and death and didn't want to admit their embarrassment. When moderns can be assured that their prayers are not irrational or run counter to natural law, but a genuine appeal to God to join with the community of faith and scientific healers in transformational healing, the prayer for healing becomes considerably more acceptable and appealing in their lives. Our renewed focus on the healing community has facilitated a prayer life for many, as they invite God into their lives to creatively face the inglorious and frightful challenges of daily living.

Shanim: Years—The Earth, Too, Is God's Creation

Bless this year for us along with all its various produce for goodness, Adonai our God,

> [*From Passover to December 4, say:* and grant blessing]

> [*From December 4 to Passover, say:* and grant dew and rain for blessing]

upon the surface of the earth, and satisfy us with its goodness, and bless our year like the best of years. Blessed are You, Adonai, who blesses our years.[7]

For our Rabbis, the Land of Israel, indeed the entire world, belongs to God, as the psalmist said, "The earth is Adonai's and all that it holds" (Psalm 24:1). The earth can be healthy or ill, a blessing or a curse, but it's all we've got. Part of God's creation and covenant, it must remain healthy for our sake. Those who observe God's commandments will continue on the Land, as we have seen. The people who refuse God's commandments will be rejected by the Land and subjected to the rule of their enemies. The Torah explains that that is the way the system works.

We've looked at two types of biblical verses. The first and most important are direct quotations from the Bible included in a prayer. The second are background quotations that clarify the Bible's attitude on the subject but are not quoted word for word in the prayer.

Atypical for Jewish prayers, and the *Tefilah* in particular, there are no direct biblical quotations in the prayer for healthy produce, the prayer termed *Shanim*, "Years." But the Bible's attitude toward the Land is essential for understanding the prayer's perspective.

The final chapters of Leviticus and Deuteronomy contain two sections of blessings and curses that result from strict adherence to Toraitic commandments: Leviticus 26 and Deuteronomy 28.

> And if, for all of that, you do not obey Me, I will go on to discipline you sevenfold for your sins, and I will break your proud glory. I will make your skies like iron and your earth like copper, so that your strength shall be spent to no purpose. Your land shall not yield its produce, nor shall the trees of the land yield their fruit.
>
> (Leviticus 26:18–20)

> But if you do not obey Adonai your God to observe faithfully all His commandments and laws which I enjoin upon you this day, all these curses shall come upon you and take effect:
>
> ... Adonai will strike you with consumption, fever, and inflammation, with scorching heat and drought, with blight and mildew; they shall hound you until you perish. The skies above your head shall be copper and the earth under you iron. Adonai will make the rain of your land dust, and sand shall drop on you from the sky, until you are wiped out.
>
> (Deuteronomy 28:15, 28:22–24)

We have all heard contemporary commentators, religious and/or political, who prophetically pronounce judgments regarding current catastrophes that, in their estimation, result directly from the public transgressing against the pundits' interpretations of biblical laws. These critics insist that God has imposed a particular current disaster, like a hurricane, as punishment for transgressing a biblical prohibition. The analyses tend not to be systematic in understanding which laws draw God's special wrath and precisely how God selects punishment. Homosexuality, for instance, seems to attract more pronouncements than murder, and abortion more than health-care failures or launching wars. Consider, for instance, this evaluation of this complex current event:

> For six days thousands of weeping people were pulled and carried from their homes. While this was taking place, a small tropical depression was forming near the Bahamas.... That small depression had turned into a frightening fiend.... Is this some sort of bizarre coincidence? Not for those who believe in the God of the Bible.... The Bible talks about Him shaking his fist over bodies of water and striking them. While the "disengagement" plan was purportedly the brainchild of Israeli Prime Minister Ariel Sharon, the United States of America has for more than a decade been the chief sponsor and propeller of a diplomatic process that has dangerously weakened Israel ... the Sharon disengagement plan was something that was forced on Israel, primarily by the United States.[8]

Pastor John Hagee, also, suggested that Hurricane Katrina was a direct divine punishment for a different sin: a gay pride parade in New Orleans.[9] Just how far will God go in naturally or supernaturally punishing transgressions by causing natural tragedy?

Considering the Consequences of Our Actions

Many would read the curses as punishments. I read them as God's built-in consequences of throwing grit into the gears of the "world machine," as we discussed earlier. We need to ask ourselves: If God is the Creator, then how does this creation actually reflect God's order? Does the creation reflect the mind of the Creator? Does a watch tell us something about the mind of the watchmaker? Are the so-called punishments simply built into creation as the consequences of refusal to mind the intricate structures of the machine? Are these punishments or simply the natural consequences of the outcome after insufficient attention to the workings of the machine? After all, even the simplest machine, if used incorrectly, will break down. If you inject too much carbon dioxide into the machine's atmosphere, is the resultant weather change a punishment or simply a built-in consequence of ignoring how the machine works, like neglecting to put oil into a car's engine? What is our human responsibility in choosing our actions as they impact the workings of God's creation? The earth is no simple apparatus. Has God created a world whose natural structure is reflected in biblical commandments and shown us how we will suffer the consequences of acting contrary to that order? Might all or parts of the Torah give us a perspective on how to maintain God's gift of the "world machine"? How do we discern which commandments work that way and which are mere cultural accretions over the centuries during which the Torah was written, reflecting the time-delimited cultures of their origin but not part of God's eternal order?

Certainly in 2016 we live in a world that is striking back at our egregious exploitation and overconsumption of the earth's resources. Does the Torah anticipate global warming, or were our ancestors attuned to living in harmony with their environment in ways we cannot even today fully appreciate? Parts of Deuteronomy 28:22–24 read like a description of California during the 2015 drought. The earth will punish as an inherent consequence of misuse, just as the Torah suggests. But are there greater factors of God's intentions at work as well?

These debates recur constantly in contemporary culture. The theological implications are debated daily in news outlets. Does the Torah forbid homosexual activities? If so, what are the consequences? Is global warming actually the consequence of ignoring Psalm 24's observation "the earth is Adonai's"?

Each believer or skeptic, you who are reading and perhaps praying this prayer, must decide personally whether your actions are part of a divine order that demands compliance and works according to natural or supernatural laws.

Did God create a world that self-adjusts to the times? Any God with sufficient intelligence to create our world would certainly build into natural law the self-corrections needed to ensure the eternal smooth functioning of the machine.

For myself, I tend to think that a Creator intelligent enough to create subatomic particles and an infinite universe that self-repairs when humans mess it up is sufficiently intelligent to create such complexity. Why would God create a world in which God has to intervene against God's own laws? Shouldn't the divine order built into the world punish those who ignore the underlying laws of God's creation? If God's creation is not self-sustaining, then that would mean that the Creator lacked either the power or the wisdom to build into the creation a system that would be self-correcting. Those course changes may occur over long expanses of time, much more than a single human life span, but God's time is not human time. As we have already seen above, "My plans are not your plans, nor are My ways your ways" (Isaiah 55:8). In short, God can afford to wait.

The prayer of "years" poses this question to each of us: are we working according to God's built-in laws that sustain the world or against those laws such that the world ultimately will reject us or our children?

Kibbutz Galuyot: Gathering the Exiles— Sound the Shofar, Blow the Horn

Sound a great shofar for our freedom, and lift up a banner to gather our exiles, and gather us together from the four corners of the earth. Blessed are You, Adonai, who gathers the dispersed among the People Israel.[10]

When both the health of the world and our personal health are perfected because we behave in accordance with the natural order of the "world machine," as reflected in God's commandments, the blast of a shofar, a ram's horn, will signal the ingathering of the dispersed of Israel from the earth's four corners, the Diaspora.

In Jewish terms the scattering of the House of Israel is part of the world's imperfection. But regardless of what you believe individually about whether God has a specific place where Jews should live, there's no doubt that many Jews ask ourselves the question of our place in the world. The utopian vision for the Jewish people states that we all will be gathered to our ancestral home, the cradle of the Jewish people, Israel.

We have avoided quoting long biblical portions. However, you may very well be familiar with the very famous Isaiah 11, the prediction that a descendant of King David will rule over Israel. This chapter is more frequently quoted by Christians than by Jews, because Christians consider it a prediction of the coming of their messiah, Jesus of Nazareth. So I am going to quote at length:

> But a shoot shall grow out of the stump of Jesse,
> A twig shall sprout from his stock.
> The spirit of Adonai shall alight upon him:
> A spirit of wisdom and insight,
> A spirit of counsel and valor,
> A spirit of devotion and reverence for Adonai.
> He shall sense the truth by his reverence for Adonai:
> He shall not judge by what his eyes behold,
> Nor decide by what his ears perceive.
> Thus he shall judge the poor with equity
> And decide with justice for the lowly of the land.
> He shall strike down a land with the rod of his
>   mouth
> And slay the wicked with the breath of his lips.
> Justice shall be the girdle of his loins,
> And faithfulness the girdle of his waist.
> The wolf shall dwell with the lamb,
> The leopard lie down with the kid;
> The calf, the beast of prey, and the fatling together,
> With a little boy to herd them.

The cow and the bear shall graze,
Their young shall lie down together;
And the lion, like the ox, shall eat straw.
A babe shall play
Over the viper's hole,
And an infant pass his hand
Over an adder's den.
In all of My sacred mount
Nothing evil or vile shall be done;
For the land shall be filled with devotion to Adonai
As the water covers the sea.

In that day
The stock of Jesse that has remained standing
Shall become a standard to peoples—
Nations shall seek his counsel
And his abode shall be honored.

In that day
My Lord will apply His hand again
To redeeming the other part of His people
From Assyria—as also Egypt, Pathros, Nubia, Elan,
    Shinar, Hamath, and the coastlands.

He will hold up a signal to the nations
And assemble the banished of Israel,
And gather the dispersed of Judah
From the four corners of the earth.

(Isaiah 11:1–12)

Here is the classic text of messianic triumph, with the dispersed of Israel gathered home. Wherever they happen to be—the ten lost tribes of Israel in modern northern Iraq, those who left for North Africa and settled in Ethiopia—all of Israel's scattered will ascend to Jerusalem and be ruled by King David's descendant.

> "As for the foreigners
> Who attach themselves to Adonai,
> To minister to Him,
> And to love the name of Adonai,
> To be His servants—
> All who keep the Sabbath and do not profane it,
> And who hold fast to My covenant—
> I will bring them to My sacred mount
> And let them rejoice in My house of prayer.
> Their burnt offerings and sacrifices
> Shall be welcome on My altar;
> For My House shall be called
> A house of prayer for all peoples."
> **Thus declares the Lord God,**
> **Who gathers the dispersed of Israel:**
> **"I will gather still more to those already**
> **gathered."**
>
> (ISAIAH 56:6–8)

How will the new age of messianic rule commence?

> And in that day **a great shofar shall be sounded**, and the strayed who are in the land of Assyria and the expelled who are in the land of Egypt shall come and worship Adonai on the holy mount, in Jerusalem.
>
> (Isaiah 27:13)

Our Rabbis saw the horn of the ram in Genesis 22, the story of "the Binding of Isaac," as being the shofar that will be sounded to inaugurate messianic time. Here's the Talmud about the role of the ram and its horn, as biblical prophet Zechariah adds his voice to Isaiah's:

> The Torah tells us: "When Abraham looked up, his eye fell upon a ram, caught in the thicket by its horns" (Genesis 22:13). This teaches us that the Holy One, blessed be God,

showed our ancestor Abraham the ram tearing himself free from one thicket and becoming entangled in another. Said the Holy One, blessed be God, to Abraham: Thus are your children destined to be caught in iniquities and entangled in misfortunes, but in the end they **will be redeemed by the horns of a ram**. Therefore the prophet Zechariah said of the time of redemption: "And Adonai will manifest Himself to them, and His arrows shall flash like lightning; my Lord God shall sound the shofar and advance in a stormy tempest" (Zechariah 9:14).

(Babylonian Talmud, *Rosh Hashanah* 16a)

The process is relatively simple, but the implications are overwhelming. God intended the world to be perfectible, and the Jewish people will assume center stage in executing God's plan.

In the last three thousand years there have been precisely three Jewish sovereign commonwealths in Israel: the First Temple period (approximately 1000–586 BCE), the Hasmonean dynasty (142–63 BCE), and the modern State of Israel. Jews dreamt and begged for a messiah to restore King David's throne and a nation to live in freedom. It was the Jewish people's fondest hope. Since 1948 we have lived with this new reality, the whisper of a reconstituted world order, the dream of redemption partially fulfilled. But many of us have failed to come to grips with its meaning.

Choosing Our Own Destiny

For those who live in the Diaspora but live constantly aware of Jewish history, this question challenges us: "Where should you spend your life: where Jews are sovereign for the third time in history, or among the nations?" For most of us the answer is one or the other, either but not both.

Certainly the messianic era of Isaiah 11 has not dawned: we do not live in a world at peace, and there is no world government from Jerusalem. Looking at the specific description of messianic time: lions are not lying down with lambs unless the lambs are for dinner, and children are not playing with vipers unless there's glass between them. Yet, many view our time period as either the beginning of end-times or simply the opportunity for Jews to live free of the world's nations while determining Jewish destiny. It's a very seductive thought: no more anti-Semitism; a country where Jews can live according to the dictates of Judaism and the Jewish conscience.

Whatever the reality of the third Jewish state, many Jews struggle with the right thing to do—for themselves, their families, and Jewish history. After being subjected to outside forces and removed from history's purview, Jews and Israel now play on history's stage and participate in determining humanity's future. That's the polar opposite from suffering the world's indifference or the cold victimization of the Nazi Holocaust. Whether an actual horn sounded or not, the Declaration of Israel's Independence on May 14, 1948, changed history for every Jew in the world.

Now the prayer reminds us daily that we choose our own destinies. Shall we live in the Land of Israel, building a modern Jewish state, as our ancestors might have chosen; or shall we live in the dispersion, as millions of Jews have done, with or without a Jewish state, since the first expulsion in 586 BCE? Which is the superior expression of Jewish life, and where will our families and we as individuals find the greatest fulfillment and add the most to the Jewish people?

Mishpat: Let Justice Run Down as Waters

Restore our judges as in days of old and our counselors as in former times. And remove sorrow and complaint from among us, and reign over us, You alone, Adonai, in kindness and mercy, and acquit us in trial. Blessed are You, Adonai, our King who loves righteousness and justice.[11]

Biblical names fascinate me. Nearly all Hebrew words originate in three-letter Hebrew roots, and the root *yod-shin-ayin* means "salvation," which is the same thing as redemption, bringing about God's purpose for the world. The biblical names Isaiah, Joshua, and Hosea all originate with these same three letters. Is the Bible hinting at the purpose of these men's lives? They are men who one way or another worked for Israel's redemption.

Isaiah is clearly the most popular of the prophets, judging by the number of haftarah readings that come from his book. The very first chapter strikes many themes that even today touch our hearts:

- The Jewish people have been disloyal to God.
- The Land of Israel was destroyed as a result of that disloyalty.
- God demands that ritual in the form of sacrifices not be divorced from social justice.
- God does not need sacrifices.
- God demands of God's people social justice as part of the covenant with God.
- Repentance is possible.
- The Jewish leadership is corrupt.

Consider what a revolutionary thought Isaiah presents: God demands that people establish justice (*mishpat*) in the world. God only provides the possibility of justice. The actual implementation resides exclusively with humans. What a thought!

Consider the culmination of Isaiah 1:

> Assuredly, this is the declaration
> Of the Sovereign, the Lord of hosts,
> The Mighty One of Israel:
> "Ah, I will get satisfaction from My foes;
> I will wreak vengeance on My enemies!
> I will turn My hand against you,
> And smelt out your dross as with lye,
> And remove all your slag:
> **I will restore your judges as in days of old,**
> **And your counselors as in former times.**
> After that you shall be called
> City of Righteousness, Faithful City."

> Zion shall be saved in the judgment;
> Her repentant ones, in the retribution.
> But rebels and sinners shall all be crushed,
> And those who forsake Adonai shall perish.
>
> (ISAIAH 1:24–28)

The Babylonian Talmud asserts that all 613 commandments in the Torah can be reduced to the eleven moral commandments in Psalm 15. By implication, all of Judaism concerns human morality. Here God is telling the prophet straight out that God does not need sacrifices from people who are acting immorally in other areas of their lives. Explicitly God demands:

> Wash yourselves clean;
> Put your evil doings
> Away from My sight.
> Cease to do evil;
> Learn to do good.
> Devote yourselves to justice;
> Aid the wronged.
> Uphold the rights of the orphan;
> Defend the cause of the widow.
>
> (ISAIAH 1:16–17)

To achieve redemption or salvation, whichever word you choose to use, we must implement divinely ordained justice through daily conduct.

The prayer continues with the request that God rule over us with kindness, mercy, righteousness, and justice. These descriptions originate in another paradisiacal vision from the prophet Hosea, a name very close to Isaiah in the original Hebrew, and with nearly the same meaning:

> In that day, I will make a covenant from them with the beasts of the field, the birds of the air, and the creeping things of the ground; I will also banish bow, sword, and war from the land. Thus I will let them lie down in safety.

And I will espouse you forever:
I will espouse you with righteousness and justice,
And with kindness and mercy,
And I will espouse you with faithfulness;
Then you shall be devoted to Adonai.

(HOSEA 2:20–22)

Included in God's righteousness and justice will be a world at peace, in which God banishes the bow, sword, and war from the land. God will be king, and humanity will live harmoniously.

These words, beginning with "And I will espouse you ...," are recited by those who don tefillin (phylacteries) for morning prayers. They are recited in part in our justice prayer, but in their entirety before morning prayers. Why? The Rabbis view the love poetry in the Song of Songs as a poem between lovers: God and Israel. How else did an otherwise pornographic book make it into the biblical canon? Indeed, the prophet Hosea speaks about Israel's infidelity to God, and he even married a prostitute to demonstrate what infidelity meant. (Prophets go a long way to prove their point!)

What are the responsibilities between spouses? At the very least, honesty and fidelity. Spouses may differ, but they aim to provide their spouse with a fulfilling life through intimate sharing. But God espouses Israel "with righteousness and justice, with kindness and mercy." How do those vows play out in our lives?

Taking Part in the March of Justice toward Salvation

Many years ago our synagogue was going to sponsor a meeting for business leaders to discuss case histories of business ethics. One business owner said to me, "What's religion got to tell me other than 'Don't do bad and do do good'?"

Of course, we were going to study case histories that would examine specific business situations in detail. Jewish law deals with the interstices of business interactions. But I think there's another, more basic function of our prayer. The greatest question is whether we desire to be part of that process and how much we are willing to risk to get there. No one wants to be the fool who does the right thing to his own disadvantage when everyone else mouths goodness and exploits the situation at every opportunity. This is what Isaiah decries at the outset of his book, that the entire nation had become corrupt. But surely we can look at the goals in Hosea and Isaiah, as implied in this justice prayer, and ask the simple question, "Are you willing to pledge to be part of this process?"

One businessman I know simply refused to deal with anyone he thought might not be entirely ethical in any of his business dealings, across the board. That was his method of preventing himself from being fleeced.

Some years ago a terrifyingly unethical pharmacist in Kansas City was caught diluting chemotherapy drugs in order to enrich himself. Many patients died as a result, and the pharmacist was jailed for his crimes.

The case was covered by the newspaper for days, and among the articles was a list of the doctors in the building who had used the pharmacist to fill prescriptions. One of my physicians had his office in that building, and I noticed he was not on the list, which seemed odd because the pharmacy was clearly the most convenient, being on the first floor of his building. Next time I saw him I asked him about it. He said, "Mark, years ago he lied to me about something, and I have kept my patients away from him ever since." He could have ignored the man's simple lie. But the fact that he intuited that his patients might not be safe likely saved lives.

What might we do to be part of the march of justice toward salvation? Is there such a thing as partial redemption, in which we take this vision of paradise and make it a partnership through our own actions? Might that process enable us to feel like we are part of something larger, helping God bring about the messianic world? Were Isaiah and Hosea alive today, how might they critique our lives? For me, all of these questions float in the background and even push their way to the foreground consciously in my prayers.

Minim: Slanderers and Heretics—Hope Is the Key

May there be no hope for slanderers, and may all wickedness instantly perish, and may all Your enemies quickly be destroyed. May

You quickly uproot, smash, destroy, and humble the insolent quickly in our day. Blessed are You, Adonai, who smashes His enemies and humbles the insolent.[12]

Sadly, the Jewish people have too often lived among enemies. Some were apostates joining another religion who attempted to harm the Jewish people to demonstrate their new loyalty. Some were simply people who didn't believe as we did and wished us harm. Obviously, those enemies spiritually impacted the Jewish people and made us wary. How do we react to wanton abuse? Do we physically fight back, or is there another, less damaging means of coping?

Rabban Gamaliel II, the Talmud reports, asked a different rabbi, Shmuel HaKatan, Samuel the Younger, to construct this prayer as an addition to the other eighteen benedictions. As Rabbi Lawrence A. Hoffman, PhD, writes, it's more of a malediction than a benediction, a visceral response to pain inflicted on the Jewish people by our enemies.[13]

The modern Reform movement has edited the prayer to condemn wickedness rather than the wicked. The Orthodox, Conservative, and Reconstructionist movements have all edited it to be more acceptable in a world in which diversity is more prized and available among Western religions. But prior to the modern world, religious acceptance was the exception rather than the norm. We can understand that, in an atmosphere of persecution, we might pray not only for the death of the sin but also for the death of the persecutor.

Some of the language of the prayer we can find in Malachi, the last of the biblical prophets. He says:

For lo! That day is at hand, burning like an oven. **All the arrogant and all the doers of evil** shall be straw, and the day that is coming—said the Lord of hosts—shall burn them to ashes and leave of them neither stock nor boughs. But for you who revere My name a sun of victory shall rise to bring healing. You shall go forth and stamp like stall-fed calves, and you shall trample the wicked to a pulp, for they shall be dust beneath your feet on the day that I am preparing—said the Lord of hosts.

>   Be mindful of the Teaching [*Torah*] of My servant Moses,
>   whom I charged at Horeb with laws and rules for all Israel.
>   Lo, I will send the prophet Elijah to you before the com-
>   ing of the awesome, fearful day of Adonai. He shall reconcile
>   parents with children and children with parents, so that, when
>   I come, I do not strike the whole land with utter destruction.
>   *Lo, I will send the prophet Elijah to you before the*
>   *coming of the awesome, fearful day of Adonai.*
>
>   (Malachi 3:19–24)

This conclusion to the prophetic book Malachi, meaning "My Messenger," foretells a different view of the messianic process. Not only will righteousness be established, but also the enemies who persecuted the Jewish people will be crushed if the people are "mindful of the Teaching [*Torah*] of My servant Moses, whom I charged at Horeb with laws and rules for all Israel."

Converting a Malediction into a Benediction

If you have a home seder at the holiday of Passover, or if you have attended seders at others' homes, you likely remember opening the door for the prophet Elijah. Elijah will announce the final redemption, first predicted here at the end of Malachi.

When the door is opened for Elijah at the seder, there appears a prayer in many Passover Haggadot that quotes Psalm 79 and is even nastier than our prayer:

>   Pour out Your fury on the nations that do not know You,
>   upon the kingdoms that do not invoke Your name,
>   for they have devoured Jacob
>   and desolated his home.
>
>   (Psalm 79:6–7)

In response to this negativity in an era of pluralism, some modern Haggadot just omit the words, assuming that we are more or less surrounded by friends today rather than enemies. But Rabbi Moshe

Hayyim Bloch composed an interesting prayer somewhere around 1963, included in some modern Haggadot, that flips the prayer on its head:

> Pour out Your love on the nations who know You
> And on kingdoms who call Your name.
> For the good which they do for the seed of Jacob
> And they shield Your People Israel from their enemies.
> May they merit to see the good of Your chosen
> And to rejoice in the joy of Your nation.[14]

The Talmud tells a story about Rabbi Meir physically threatened by outlaws. To rid himself of the peril, Rabbi Meir decides to pray for their demise. But his scholarly wife, Bruria, quotes Psalm 104:35, "May sinners disappear from the earth, and the wicked be no more," and suggests to her spiritually connected and brilliant husband that he should pray for the end of the sinning rather than the death of the sinners. He does, the marauders repent, and Rabbi Meir's life becomes easier without exchanging hatred.

In the mid-1990s Rabbi Michael Weisser converted the leader of the KKK in Nebraska to Judaism. Weisser is a modern-day Bruria. Rabbi Weisser accomplished this amazing feat by calling the man once a week and offering love rather than hatred.[15] Certainly such outreach in kindness does not always work, but how amazing to try! We might pray, in accordance with Psalm 104, that through our deeds the sinners will disappear from the earth not because they die but because they alter their beliefs and behaviors. And in accord with Bruria and Rabbi Weisser's intentions, perhaps that can be a result of our actions.

Sometimes our spirituality enables us to express less than gracious sentiments and perhaps to convert a malediction into a benediction. Our prayer releases some bile resulting from persecution. One role of prayer, as we witness here, is to enable us to examine our own viscera and determine our reactions to the ways we are treated in the world. The world is often not kind. Prayer helps us be agents of God in *tikkun olam*, repairing the world. Perhaps, along this trail to a new, more messianic reality, we can examine the roles we play in the journey to a more perfected world.

Tzadikim: For the Righteous, the Pious, the Converts, and the Rest of Us—Trusting in God

Show compassion to the righteous, to the pious, to the leaders of Your People, the House of Israel, to the remnants of their sages, to righteous converts, and to us, Adonai our God. And give a good reward to all who truly trust in Your name, and let our lot be among them forever that we will not be shamed, for we put our trust in You. Blessed are You, Adonai, who is the support and trust of the righteous.[16]

Having prayed that God cut off hope from God's enemies, we now flip to the positive side of the coin: reward for the righteous (*tzadikim*).

Once again no direct biblical quotations appear in the prayer, but, as Rabbi David Abudraham (fourteenth-century Spain) points out, we have ample biblical precedent for the topics.

The previous prayer banished hope for slanderers and sought that the wicked perish while God's enemies are destroyed. Now we turn to categories of those loyal to God: the righteous, the pious, the leaders of the people, the remnants of the sages, righteous converts, and the rest of us who may not share in the pure goodness of the other categories.

Setting the tone, the prayer opens with the righteous, which appears in Psalm 34:

> Come, my sons, listen to me;
> I will teach you what it is to fear Adonai.
> Who is the man who is eager for life,
> who desires years of good fortune?
> Guard your tongue from evil,
> your lips from deceitful speech.
> Shun evil and do good,
> seek amity [*shalom*] and pursue it.
> The eyes of Adonai are on **the righteous**,
> His ears attentive to their cry.
>
> (PSALM 34:12–16)

I would translate the second line above as "I will teach you about reverence for Adonai." The Hebrew better reflects the English concept of reverence, a positive emotion, rather than fear, which is negative. Here again we see the centrality of ethical conduct to achieving the messianic time. The righteous shun evil and do good, and therefore God's eyes and ears are attentive to them.

In Psalm 34 we view many of the qualities of a righteous person: eager for life, does not slander others, speaks the truth, desires the good and shuns evil, and seeks peace. The types of people listed in our prayer seem to all be included in those qualities, although they fall into different categories. The categories are not well defined. They are simply the people who follow God's path.

Second-century sage Rabbi Ishmael taught that the Torah speaks in human language. We can apply that to the psalm here as well. No, God does not have eyes and ears, but you get the idea: God's senses, so to speak, are trained on the righteous for reward. There are various kinds of totally good people, and some are listed in the prayer.

The Mishnah's author, Judah the Prince, nicknamed simply "Rabbi," closed out the practical tractates of the Mishnah with basic principles, called *Pirkei Avot*. Call it "the big picture." The title translates to "Chapters of the Fathers," but I translate it as "The Chapters of Basic Principles." *Avot* puns as both "basic principles" and "fathers."

Pirkei Avot 4:2 observes, "Ben Azai says, 'Be quick to obey a minor mitzvah as a major one, and flee from transgression: for one mitzvah performed leads to another, and one transgression leads to another....'" We often describe Judaism as a religion of laws, but that's a myopic view. Rather, Judaism's legislative cornucopia persistently connects us to God and thereby living righteously every moment. Reciting a minimum of one hundred blessings daily, connecting to God through a *b'rakhah* (liturgical blessing) whenever we have an appetite, thinking constantly of "what does Adonai require of me?" (Micah 6:8) brings the average person closer to a righteous life not as a philosophical proposition but as moment by lived moment: like an angel of goodness perched on our right shoulders, constantly whispering in our ears.

These are the better angels of our nature, and when they work as intended, they distance us from our selfish desires and make us aware that we live in two worlds simultaneously: one physical and the other spiritual. For successful living, Judaism points insistently to the spiritual world and asks, "Are you in compliance with both worlds?" Ben Azai said it best, "Doing one mitzvah pulls another in its wake," and transgressions do the same.

I taught one Yom Kippur morning about not being so self-centered in our day-to-day dealings with the world. About a week later I ran into a very intelligent, highly successful congregant who has little use for Judaism. He said this to me: "You know, I listened to your sermon on Yom Kippur morning, and as soon as you were done, I left. I jumped into my car and headed to the mall to pick up something I needed. It was very crowded, and a parking space was just opening and I was going to take it, but someone beat me to it. I was about to yell at them, but then I thought, 'Nope, too soon after the sermon.' So I let it go."

We humans often require an external voice that calls us to the best within us.

Many forces argue against doing the right thing. But the prayer for the righteous encourages us to desire to count ourselves among them, and "one mitzvah pulls another" in its wake.

Jewish cosmology contends that the universe works best when righteousness rules the day. God, therefore, sets God's mind on the righteous and even potentially rewards them. The psalm goes on to say:

> Adonai is close to the brokenhearted;
> those crushed in spirit He delivers.
> Though the misfortunes of the righteous be many,
> Adonai will save him from them all,
> keeping all his bones intact,
> not one of them being broken.
> One misfortune is the deathblow of the wicked;
> the foes of the righteous shall be ruined.
> Adonai redeems the life of his servants;
> all who take refuge in Him shall not be ruined.
>
> (PSALM 34:19–23)

We find a pious hope that the life of the righteous wins out in the end, that the wicked do not triumph.

The Rabbis, through a grammatically based reinterpretation of a Hebrew root, construe each appearance of the word "stranger" (*ger*) in the Torah as meaning "convert." Therefore, Deuteronomy 10:19, "You shall love the stranger, for you were strangers in the land of Egypt," is understood to refer to converts to Judaism. This same idea is repeated over thirty times in the Torah, taken by the Rabbis to express acceptance toward those who choose of their own volition to join the House of Israel, rather than the biblical intention of welcoming the non-Israelite stranger.

The Hebrew word for "pious" is *hasid*, which is used in various ways. In Psalm 86:2 the *hasid* is translated as "steadfast":

> Incline Your ear, Adonai,
> answer me,
> for I am poor and needy.
> Preserve my life, **for I am steadfast [*hasid*]**;
> O You, my God,
> **deliver Your servant who trusts in You.**
> Have mercy on me, O Lord,
> for I call to You all day long;
> bring joy to Your servant's life,
> for on You, Lord, I set my hope.
> For You, Lord, are good and forgiving,
> abounding in steadfast love to all who call on You.
> Give ear, Adonai, to my prayer;
> heed my plea for mercy.
> In my time of trouble I call You,
> for You will answer me.
>
> (PSALM 86:1–7)

These sentiments are very nearly those in our prayer, "And give a good reward to all who truly trust in Your name, and let our lot be among them forever that we will not be shamed, for we put our trust in You." God's goodness and quality of forgiveness enable us to believe that God will reward and give a place with God to those who trust in the Divine Presence. The same sentiment can be found in Psalm 9:11, "Those who know Your name trust You, for You do not abandon those who turn to You, Adonai."

Why do bad things happen to good people, and good things to bad people? Theodicy presents the greatest challenge to religion and a moral God: why do the righteous suffer and the wicked prosper? In a perfect world, righteousness would triumph over evil. But, in the real world, the good sometimes suffer unmercifully because the world is unredeemed. When the messianic triumphs over the wicked order that rules today, then the orderliness of creation will make sense, as originally intended in the Garden of Eden, and pristine goodness will be restored to the world.

Yet evil does serve a purpose; it reminds us by contrast of how good we have it. I live in a very prosperous county. When people have petty complaints, forgetting the luxury enveloping them, I am known to say, "You know what I tell myself? If yesterday I was in Auschwitz, how bad is today?" As the kabbalists teach, even pain and evil can be turned into a blessing with the proper perspective.

Yerushalayim: Return to Jerusalem— Homecoming to Where I've Never Been

Return to Jerusalem Your city in compassion, and dwell in its midst as You promised You would, and rebuild it soon in our day into an eternal structure, and quickly establish David's throne within it. Blessed are You, Adonai, who rebuilds Jerusalem.[17]

When justice is established, the wicked are destroyed, and the righteous are rewarded, then God will rebuild God's home in Jerusalem.

We have already seen that God resides everywhere—"The earth is Adonai's and all that it holds" (Psalm 24:1)—and yet, God possesses a special indwelling presence on the Temple Mount in Jerusalem.

God commands the building of a Tabernacle during Israel's forty Sinai wilderness years, a period of time in a place where God could focus and intensify God's presence: "And let them make Me a sanctuary that I may dwell among them" (Exodus 25:8).

The Hebrew word translated as "dwell" derives from the three-letter Hebrew root *shin-khaf-nun* (*sh-kh-n*). "To dwell" is *shakhan*, but many people are familiar with the noun form, which becomes the name of the aspect of God that dwells on earth, *Shekhinah*, utilizing the same three Hebrew root letters.

Our prayer says, "Return to Your city Jerusalem in compassion, and dwell in it as You promised You would," a clear reference first to the wilderness Tabernacle, which contained the two tablets of the Ten Commandments, and then to the catchphrase in the book of Deuteronomy, "the place where I will cause my name to dwell," which appears six times in that book alone.

> Observe the month of Abib and offer a passover sacrifice to Adonai your God, for it was in the month of Abib, at night, that Adonai your God freed you from Egypt. You shall slaughter the passover sacrifice for Adonai your God, from the flock or the herd, **in the place where** Adonai **will choose to establish His name**....
>
> You are not permitted to slaughter the passover sacrifice in any of the settlements that Adonai your God is giving you; **but at the place where** Adonai **your God will choose to establish His name**, there alone shall you slaughter the passover sacrifice, in the evening, at sundown, the time of day when you departed from Egypt....
>
> Three times a year—on the Feast of Unleavened Bread, on the Feast of Weeks, and on the Feast of Booths—all your males shall appear **before Adonai your God in the place that He will choose**.
>
> (Deuteronomy 16:1–2, 16:5–6, 16:16)

The word "dwell" in our prayer implies the presence of the same divine aspect that occupied the Tabernacle while Israel traveled in the wilderness and ultimately took up residence in Solomon's Temple on Mount

Moriah, the Temple Mount. You may be familiar with the film version
of the search for the Ark of the Covenant, the movie *Raiders of the Lost
Ark*, by Steven Spielberg. Jews consider the Holy of Holies in the Temple
to be the holiest place on the globe because God concentrated divine
holiness there. When the magnificent Herodian Second Temple was
destroyed, the myth became that the *Shekhinah* withdrew heavenward.
The rebuilding of the Temple will reestablish God's sacred presence on
earth, and specifically in God's holy city, Jerusalem.

> Aliens shall **rebuild your walls**,
> Their kings shall wait upon you—
> For in anger I struck you down,
> But in favor I take you back.
> Your gates shall always stay open—
> Day and night they shall never be shut—
> To let in the wealth of the nations,
> With their kings in procession.
>
> For the nation or the kingdom
> That does not serve you shall perish;
> Such nations shall be destroyed ...
>
> Bowing before you, shall come
> The children of those who tormented you;
> Prostrate at the soles of your feet
> Shall be those who reviled you;
> And you shall be called
> "City of Adonai,
> Zion of the holy One of Israel."
>
> (ISAIAH 60:10–12, 60:14)

The Jewish people must be restored to both God and God's historic Land
of Israel, reinstating God's presence on the Temple Mount, "the place
where God will cause His name to dwell." As I write this, Israelis and
Palestinians are disputing that very mountain as the religious and political

struggles merge and find expression in control of the geographical area over which wars have been fought for three thousand years, since David conquered the city and made it his capital around 1000 BCE. In Isaiah's vision, written in Babylonian captivity, after the destruction of the First Temple and awaiting the return, Jerusalem's former glory will be restored economically and politically. The Jewish people will be reinstated in their previous status with God, and God's capital city, Jerusalem, will assume its prior glory, where God's presence, the *Shekhinah*, will abide.

David had wanted and offered to build God's house, but according to the Bible, God denied him the privilege, which instead went to David's son, Solomon. Many of the elements of our prayer are contained in this account of the dedication of Solomon's Temple:

> When the priests came out of the sanctuary—for the cloud had filled the House of Adonai ... for the Presence of Adonai filled the House of Adonai—then Solomon declared:
>
> "... I have now built for You
> A stately House,
> A place where You
> May dwell forever."

> Then, with the whole congregation of Israel standing, the king faced about and blessed the whole congregation of Israel. He said:
>
> "Praised be Adonai, the God of Israel, who has fulfilled with deeds the promise He made to my father, David. For he said, 'Ever since I brought My People Israel out of Egypt, I have not chosen a city among all of the tribes of Israel for building a House where My name might abide, but I have chosen David to rule My People Israel.'
>
> "Now my father David had intended **to build a House** for the name of Adonai, the God of Israel. But Adonai said to my father, David, 'As regards your intention to build a House for My name, you did right to have that intention. However, you

shall not build the House yourself; instead, your son, the issue of your loins, shall build the House for My name.'

"And Adonai has fulfilled the promise that He made: I have succeeded my father David and ascended the **throne of Israel**, as Adonai promised. I have built the House for the name of Adonai, the God of Israel, and **I have set a place there for the Ark, containing the covenant**, which Adonai made with our fathers when He brought them out of the land of Egypt."

(1 Kings 8:10–19)

King Solomon carried out the eternal promise to the prophet Samuel:

Adonai declares to you that He, Adonai, **will establish a house for you**. When your days are done and you lie with your fathers, I will raise up your offspring after you, one of your own issue, and I will establish his kingship. He shall build a house for My name, and **I will establish his royal throne forever**.... Your house and your kingship shall ever be secure before you; **your throne shall be established forever**.

(2 Samuel 7:11–13, 7:16)

God's presence in the Ark of the Covenant existed for over twelve hundred years, an extremely long period, with only a brief seventy-year hiatus, while in Babylonian exile. According to the biblical account in the wilderness, and then the traditions of the First and Second Temple, which the people had seen with their own eyes, the Ark existed on the Temple Mount once Solomon completed the Temple. This holiest place in the world connected the Jewish people to God on earth and Jewish history for over a millennium. We can understand the idea of God's promised reestablishment of Jerusalem, the Temple Mount, and the Temple as a verifiable ideal with a factual history, given the covenant between the Jewish people and their God on that very place.

This process of exile, return, and rebuilding had happened before. Not only did Isaiah predict it, but the prophet Zechariah was part of it between 520 and 515 BCE:

> Thus said the Lord of hosts: I will rescue My people from the lands of the east and from the lands of the west, and I will bring them home to dwell in Jerusalem. They shall be My people, and I will be their God—in truth and sincerity.
>
> (Zechariah 8:7–8)

Therefore, given the wilderness experience, the transfer of the Ark of the Covenant to the First Temple, then the continuation after exile into the Second Temple, why would they doubt the process? The *Tefilah* lays out what will happen again, after the Roman destruction, in Rabbi Gamaliel II's time or after, which will culminate in the reestablishment of the Temple and the cult and, finally, the seating of King David's descendant on the throne of the Davidic dynasty. Certainly this complete restoration is a worthy subject of prayer for the House of Israel daily at the very times when the *tamid*, the daily sacrifice, was offered, maintaining Israel's covenant with God in the absence of that sacrifice.

Today, with the reestablishment of a Jewish State in Israel for only the third time in three millennia, naturally the same messianic fervor effervesces among segments of the world Jewish population. Nineteen centuries of prayer-inspired hopefulness, often amidst persecution, have funneled down to our day. The messiah's imminent arrival, expected among portions of both Jewish and Christian populations, creates an often tumultuous expectation that the end-times are upon us, and raises an anticipation that God's presence will soon appear on the Temple Mount. The resulting hopes increase both religious fervor and political conflict.

Israel's rise presents our generation with a gift and a challenge: to appreciate our good fortune and responsibility to participate in fulfilling the biblical vision of God's kingdom for all peoples, and to ensure that the hope of *Shekhinah's* return completes the messianic vision of a world at peace.

David: King David Blossoms on Jerusalem's Throne

Cause the progeny of David, Your servant, to blossom quickly. Let him shine in Your deliverance, for we await Your salvation every day. Blessed are You, Adonai, who causes the light of salvation to blossom.[18]

The way is prepared. Jerusalem is rebuilt, and the throne awaits the king. The People Israel are intended by God to live under God's reign, but a millennium earlier God allowed them to have a human king who would serve God and the people, an intermediary of sorts to facilitate God's rule on earth.

We have already witnessed Isaiah 11 above (seventh blessing, *Kibbutz Galuyot*), which opens with the image of David as a planting growing from his father, Jesse:

> But a shoot shall grow out of the stump of Jesse,
> A twig shall sprout from his stock.
>
> (ISAIAH 11:1)

Now Jeremiah extends that image:

> See, a time is coming—declares Adonai—when I will raise up **a true branch of David's line** [*tzemach tzadik*]. He shall **reign as king** and shall prosper, and he shall do what is **just and right in the land**. In his days Judah shall be delivered and Israel shall dwell secure. And this is the name by which he shall be called: "Adonai is our Vindicator."
>
> (Jeremiah 23:5–6)

Translations are often curious things, and it's difficult to know how others read a text unless they tell you. The *JPS Tanakh* translates *tzemach tzadik* as "a true branch," when we previously saw the word *tzadik* translated as "righteous." Of course, the blessing regarding Slanderers and Heretics (see "Converting a Malediction into a Benediction," above) promised righteousness, which would be a result of having a righteous king, descendant of David. This verse could have been translated as "righteous branch." The word "Vindicator" here, *tzidkeinu*, also comes from the same Hebrew root letters and could similarly be translated consistently as "righteous one."

See, days are coming—declares Adonai—when I will fulfill the promise that I made concerning the House of Israel and the House of Judah. In those days and at that time, **I will raise up** [*atzmiach*—the same Hebrew root as "progeny" and "blossom" in our prayer] **a true branch of David's line**, and **he shall do what is just and right in the land**. In those days Judah shall be delivered and Israel shall dwell secure. And this is what she shall be called: "Adonai is our Vindicator." For thus said Adonai: **There shall never be an end to men of David's line who sit upon the throne of the House of Israel**.

(Jeremiah 33:14–17)

Interestingly, whereas Jeremiah preaches before the Babylonian calamities in 603 BCE and 586 BCE, he foresees what's coming and informs the king. Jeremiah is brutally honest, foreseeing the destruction, and yet this prophecy is meant to bring comfort that regardless of the approaching nightmare, Israel will not ultimately be abandoned by God.

That same comfort is now extended to the identical historical community many centuries later and in the same words, at least through employing the same imagery. Those praying these words would be comforted not only by the pleasant thought, but also by the assurance that in the previous cataclysmic crisis, which also destroyed the Temple, the final outcome restored the kingdom, if not the actual Davidic dynasty. The Temple and its sacrificial system maintaining the covenant with God were rebuilt, and the promise could still be fulfilled that David's descendants would again occupy the throne and restore the glory.

The words of the prophet Hosea from the eighth century BCE may have provided comfort to post–70 CE Jews, however, who longed for a vanished descendant of David, which had not occurred for over five hundred years. Hosea preached:

For the Israelites shall go a long time without a king and without officials, without sacrifice and without cult pillars, and without ephod and teraphim. Afterward, the Israelites will turn

back and will **seek Adonai their God and David their king—**
and they will thrill over Adonai and over His bounty in the
days to come.

(Hosea 3:4–5)

Their hope and expectations were not only that God would not abandon
God's people, but also that God's relationship to Israel was eternal, and
that past restorations would be repeated after Israel repented her sins.

In 1969, two years after the miraculous Six-Day War (see the
first blessing, "Knowledge"), as the American study abroad program at
Hebrew University in Jerusalem expanded dramatically and Jerusalem
itself spread geographically, I, along with many friends, took my junior
year of college abroad at Hebrew University. Several among us determined to stay, and have lived their lives and raised their children as
Israelis, determining the destiny of the Jewish people from inside the
Jewish homeland. I chose to return to the United States and become a
rabbi, and for the last four decades have served the Jewish people in a
different way. Now I get to look back over the decisions that we made.
They were fateful for us all.

Clearly the governance of the Jewish people has been critical to
the events that have transpired. Just witness the conflict over Israel's
nearly fifty-year occupation of the West Bank, so controversial in daily
events not only in the Middle East but also around the world. Among
North American Jewry, in Israel, and around the world, Jewish leadership has become a major protagonist in the human drama. One only
need read the newspapers to see how the return to Israel's homeland and
the choice of leadership shapes lives worldwide, for better or for worse.
Israel has returned to the world stage after nineteen hundred years.

Most remarkably, the continued existence of *Am Yisrael*, the People
Israel, whose demise was not only predicted but also at times actively
sought by other Abrahamic faiths or other nations, was never in doubt
by most Jews. Yet, will God send a Redeemer to save the Jewish people
and establish peace in the world? I have my doubts, but about this I am
certain: our obligation to fulfill the prophetic vision of peace among the
nations is the modern application of Isaiah's vision and rests collectively

upon us all. Israel's founders refused to wait longer for divine intervention and redemption, and therefore determined to act. One prominent member of Israel's political class even wrote that had his grandfather's generation chosen to accept Britain's Uganda Plan, perhaps millions of Europe's Jews could have been saved from the Holocaust.[19] Political decision making matters dramatically in real lives.

The *Tefilah* places the Jewish people squarely in the center of human history. We have just witnessed in prayer a detailed plan for the process of world redemption. It is doubtful that the world's destiny will rest upon a descendant of the Davidic dynasty crowned king. Yet, these prayers raise the question: Does the renewed Jewish people matter to the fate of the planet and its population? Without a doubt! And each of us chooses to play a role in or ignore this promise made millennia ago that has somehow come to fruition in our own time. The result is as miraculous as the prediction made four thousand years ago that Abraham's descendants would be a blessing to humanity, and certainly no Jew can ignore the challenge to decide his or her role. Perhaps it is ironic that in an age of extreme individualism, the collective has come to make such a difference for the world.

Israel's founders and visionaries altered the world's destiny, but it has fallen to us as our obligation to ensure that the end result fulfills the prophetic vision. That is what the generation immediately following the Six-Day War set out to do, although perhaps without entirely realizing its importance. By studying in Israel we fulfilled our internal impulse that lives must make a difference and we have a shared role to play in the history of the Jewish people. I daresay that this simple decision changed us all, and in some cases, the destiny of our people. The Mishnah teaches, "It's not your obligation to complete the task; but neither are you free of it altogether" (*Mishnah Avot* 2:21). That was the assigned topic of my Confirmation Class essay in 1965. And Hillel said, "If I am not for myself who will be for me? If I am only for myself what am I? And, if not now, when?" (Ibid., 1:14). The *Tefilah* is not just rote prayers. They are also a prophetic vision of the constituent elements of a messianic world yet to be created, a paradisiacal vision of what might be if we accept the challenge "to perfect the world under the sovereignty of God" (the *Aleynu* prayer, prior to Mourner's Kaddish, daily service). The biblical story teaches us: God created a perfect world, but humans messed it up. Our job, in partnership with God, is to restore God's original perfection.

The process of redemption is complete. All that remains is to pray that God hear our prayerful voices and be merciful and munificent in granting our requests, demonstrating that God does, indeed, hear our supplications.

Tefilah: Prayer—God, Are You Listening?

Hear our voice, Adonai our God. Have pity and mercy on us, and accept our prayer with favor, for You are the God who hears our prayers and supplications. Do not turn us away from You, our Ruler, empty-handed, for You hear the prayer of Your People Israel in mercy. Blessed are You, Adonai, who hears prayer.[20]

We now complete the thirteen petitions describing the process of the reconstruction of God's kingdom on earth, the movement of Israel from defeated sinner nation to reconstituted servant of God. We began with God's granting knowledge, discernment, and understanding to God's people. Then we moved to blessings for Jewish repentance and divine forgiveness. Finally, starting with a blessing for the possibility of redemption, we recounted the steps in building the messianic coming. We've prayed a description of the events leading to reestablishing the Davidic dynasty on the throne in Jerusalem.

The *Tefilah*, the core prayer of Jewish worship, was composed in its entirety to substitute for the daily sacrifice. The individual prayers, taken separately, each describe a part of the process of redemption; but simultaneously, considered together, they act to represent the House of Israel before God. We witness, therefore, the complexity of Jewish worship as the same words play different roles simultaneously in drawing closer to the Divine.

Add to that the intertextual use of biblical quotations, through which an entire biblical story is imported into the meaning within the prayer by simply using a few words of the story to represent its totality. We see that Jewish prayer is a series of parts working in harmony and separately, like a complex poem, to generate meaning in the life of the praying person.

In this last of the petitionary prayers, we request that God interact with Israel by mercifully hearing the petitions and accepting them as God previously accepted sacrifice. A prior rubric in Jewish worship, the *Shema* and Its Blessings, portrays the Jewish people as a hearing people, by quoting Deuteronomy 6:4, "Hear, O Israel: Adonai is our God; Adonai is One." Now, in this final petition, we pray that God is likewise a hearing God who hearkens to God's people's supplications. The earthly people and their heavenly God are acknowledged reciprocally by words. But not just any words. Israel connects with God through quotations originating in God's scripture. Sacred scripture is the text shared by God and God's people, capturing the Divine-human encounter. The nexus between the Divine and the human comes through words originating both in God's revealed text and in God's people, with prayerful recitation of holy words and concepts causing melding between the two. The power of prayer is therefore a process of bringing together the confluence of divine writ and soulful hope to elevate the human spirit to achieve divine aspirations through sacred words. We witness here a partnership between God and the people, between divine wisdom and creaturely hope to live in a kingdom fulfilling God's own vision for peace on earth.

Psalm 5:3 is very similar, although not directly quoted in our prayer:

> Give ear to my speech, Adonai;
> consider my utterance.
> Heed the sound of my cry,
> my King and God,
> **for I pray to You.**
> **Hear my voice, Adonai**, at daybreak;
> at daybreak I plead before You, and wait.
>
> (PSALM 5:2–4)

Verse 3 can be translated, "Listen [*hakshivah*] to the voice of my cry, my King and my God, for to You I pray." The word "pray," *etpalal*, is a form of the word *Tefilah*, the Rabbinic name both for this prayer and for the entirety of the nineteen benedictions. Further, the prayer occurs at daybreak, as did the morning sacrifice and the *Tefilah* prayer that replaced it.

Psalm 4:2 asks God to "hear my *Tefilah*," again the name of both this prayer and the entire nineteen benedictions. The psalm sounds very much like Jeremiah 23, which we saw in the discussion of the previous prayer:

> Answer me when I call,
> O God, my vindicator!
> You freed me from distress;
> have mercy on me and hear my prayer.
>
> (PSALM 4:2)

The psalm actually quoted in our prayer is the following:

> Praise befits You in Zion, O God;
> vows are paid to You;
> all mankind comes to You,
> **You who hear prayer.**
> When all manner of sins overwhelm me,
> it is You who forgives our iniquities.
> Happy is the man You choose and bring near
> to dwell in Your courts;
> may we be sated with the blessings of Your house,
> Your holy Temple.
>
> (PSALM 65:2–5)

God receives the praise of the people through prayer in Zion, where the Temple will be rebuilt. God hears prayer and forgives the sins of God's people, Israel, which caused the destruction of the Temple. Israel needs God's mercy and forgiveness, and this final prayer pleads that the prayers be accepted with the goal of redeeming the exile of Israel from their God and restoration of God's rule on earth. The Temple will be restored, and God's blessings will return the Jewish people to God's sacred courts in the Temple in the holy city of Jerusalem.

I write while an unresolved politico-religious controversy rages in Israel and North America over egalitarian prayer access to the Western Wall, the *Kotel Ha-Ma'aravi*. In recent decades, proximity to the ancient Temple site has been politicized beyond anyone's expectations. When the Wall was recaptured in the 1967 war, for the first time in nineteen years the Jewish people could access the central shrine of Jewish life. Now that shrine has become the centerpiece in a political and cultural power struggle.

But, prayer at the Western Wall does not move every Jew. It's proximity to ancient ideas of holiness does not touch most lives. I, for instance, reflecting on dozens of times I have visited the Temple Mount and Western Wall, remain unmoved spiritually, while historically connected. It is a symbol, not an actual nexus between God and *Amkha* (the Jewish people).

Yet the ideal of national restoration has progressed farther than most would have thought possible just a century ago. The Temple Mount symbolizes that this achievement is not merely political, but spiritual and historical as well. Israel does not represent simply a haven, but also the historic *axis mundi* of a people who for millennia has aspired to be in God's favor and to even fulfill God's wishes on earth. The Temple Mount represents so much more than sacrifices or even national aspirations, so much more than safety from persecution. For Jews it symbolizes the possibility of linking our lives to God's purpose, both for individuals and for humanity. It represents, therefore, the aspiration to divinely guided human fulfillment and, simultaneously, to national restoration.

When we pray, we ask, along with the psalmists, that God "hear" our prayer. It's not important where the prayers are uttered or if we are just moving our lips as Hannah did at this same location (I Samuel 1). We face the Temple Mount in prayer because all of these humanitarian, national, individual, and historical aspirations coalesce in a single, unique location, symbolized by the *Tefilah*. The heart and soul of the Jewish people, their hopes and dreams, have been uttered imagining this place. Whatever its religious status, the Western Wall unites the Jewish people over time and location. It is not a praying space but an ideal of the fulfillment of God's purpose for God's people. I have felt this countless times when standing at the Wall or in the Kotel courtyard. And yet, I would relinquish it in a second if to share this sacred space would bring peace to our people, the Middle East, and our world.

"The earth is the Lord's and the fullness thereof, the world and they who dwell therein" (Psalm 24:1). We Jews may imagine and aspire to Jerusalem when we pray, but we access God equally from wherever we turn in prayer. As Rabbi Menachem Mendel of Kotzk said, "Where is God? Wherever you let God in."

The Intermediate
Blessings for Shabbat
and Festivals

Kedushat HaYom—
The Holiness of the Day

All time is not the same. In college French class I literally counted down minute by minute the ninety minutes I sat in class. I never counted down the time on a Saturday night date. Well, just once. Social time sped by like cars on a racetrack; French class time crept by like watching a worm cross a country road.

In American life we don't exactly talk about holy time. In the American secular holiday calendar, however, we do have special times that feel different than everyday time. Thanksgiving reaches nearly religious stature. Christmas Day, even for non-Christians who perhaps get the day off of work and use it as a family-together time, elicits gratitude and joy. Birthdays and other anniversaries, along with New Year's Eve, assume exalted positions in the American calendar, eliciting memorable celebrations. But none claims holiness.

The day before I wrote this, Greater Kansas City, where I live, celebrated a World Series Victory Day, and literally 40 percent of the metropolitan area residents, reportedly 800,000 people, gathered in the center city to celebrate. No crime occurred. There were no arrests. Nearly a million people rejoiced together, with many more joining in the civic glee by watching on television at home. The entire metropolitan area of 2.03 million people came together as one; schools closed and businesses shut down. Kansas City celebrated the best holiday ever, uniting both sides of the indomitable Missouri-Kansas state line politically separating the two-state area, and the instrument of unity was a baseball series! Time changed; but as much as the community united and time altered its feel, we did not access the holy.

Sacred time differs in religious cosmology from secular time. In sacred time, limited humans gain access to God's infinity and perhaps even experience a taste of eternity. Scientific measuring of nanoseconds doesn't change, but time feels different. Much of that change is accomplished through prayer.

Introduction to the Intermediate Blessing for Erev Shabbat: Humanity at the Center of God's Intention

You sanctified the seventh day for Your name, as the end of the creation of heaven and earth, and You blessed it beyond all other days and sanctified it beyond all other times, as is written in Your Torah:

Heaven and the earth and everything associated with them were completed. On the seventh day, God completed the work He had done. On the seventh day, He rested from all the work He had done. God blessed the seventh day and sanctified it, for on it He rested from all the work God created to do.[1]

Certain passages of Torah many Jews know by heart in Hebrew and hold dear. Certainly the *Shema*, Deuteronomy 6:4, springs first to mind. But somewhere in there, right up near the top of the list, we'll find Genesis 2:1–3, "*Vayekhulu hashamayim v'haaretz v'khol tz'vaam ...*" (**Heaven and the earth and everything associated with them were completed ...**), best known as the opening of the Friday night sanctification (*Kiddush*) over the wine.

Likely the most important reason so many people know this by heart is that it's recited three times on Friday night, Erev Shabbat, both in synagogue and at home. One of those times is during the intermediate blessing of the *Tefilah* on Erev Shabbat. Because these Torah verses double as the introduction to the home *Kiddush*, sung while beloved family and friends surround the Shabbat dinner table to bless the wine, our passage is likely to connect to heartwarming family memories.

Most of the Bible quotations in the prayers we have considered in previous chapters are brief, often just several words. But here we find three complete verses introducing a prayer. As we might anticipate, the verse selection brings a special message.

The opening three blessings of the *Tefilah* are together often called Blessings of Praise, with their individual themes being the merit of our ancestors, God's might, and God's holiness. Those three are followed on weekdays by the thirteen individual petitions we studied in the previous chapter, detailing the process of redemption and the coming of the messianic descendant of King David. But should we pray the same thirteen blessings on biblically commanded Sabbaths and festivals?

Tradition teaches that the Sabbath is for rest and therefore an inappropriate time to petition God. Let God rest! Enough with the requests! Don't be a noodge.

But there's another, perhaps more important factor: Sabbaths and festivals are intrinsically holy. They feel different, the way birthdays felt different when we were children. They are special time, and for families who create a day that is "a taste of the world to come," time feels distinctive, overflowing with happy memories. The Torah commands their observance, and their holiness is embedded as part of creation. Because these days are inherently different, some of the associated prayers are different as well.

The intermediate blessings for Sabbaths and festivals each have separate introductory quotations from the Bible, followed in each instance by the same continuation of the prayer celebrating the holiness of the day. Although the *Kedushat HaYom* prayer in each service—evening, morning, additional, afternoon, and festivals—differs by biblical quotations, they are the same because the final part of each is identical.

Beginning with Erev Shabbat, we open with verses that complete the first Creation story in Genesis. Shabbat is described as the pinnacle, the final and ultimate act of God's creation. In interpreting the first verse, the Babylonian Talmud (*Shabbat* 119b) alters the vowels in the first word to indicate that people and God collaborated to complete creation together rather than God alone, and therefore they paused for rest from their combined activity. That minor vowel change, sanctioned because the Torah scroll is written without vowels, implies a joint venture between humans and God in creating the world. In effect, our human purpose becomes partnering in completing God's creation.

The idea that humans complete divine design in harmony with God provides a profoundly moving modus operandi in Judaism. For instance, circumcision, commanded for all male descendants of Abraham in Genesis 17, is not framed in Jewish thinking as a removal of a part of the body, but instead of perfecting what came into the world incomplete. This may seem curious, but it's a method of including humanity as co-creators with the Eternal rather than just another creation. No other animal participates with God as demi-creators. It brings substance to the vague idea that mortals are "a little less than divine" (Psalm 8:6), more like angels than animals. We have a role to play in the destiny of the world, and as a result we can conclude that every life possesses significance because it has the potential to impact all of creation, although we may often feel minute and insignificant in the greater scheme of things.

This ennobling idea is an antidote to the modern existential affliction of personal insignificance, found so frequently in Western culture and art. In Jewish cosmology, regardless of what kind of job you happen to occupy (think Arthur Miller's *Death of a Salesman*), you have disproportionate significance because your actions affect God's cosmos and embrace you in completing the world. This is not Pollyannaish. Our lives are too short to appreciate their impact. You and I cannot determine whose lives we have touched, in what manner, and with what result. It takes many decades to play out, and even then we'll not be able to discern. Add to that this notion that we share with God on a cosmic level, and our ultimate impact cannot possibly be deciphered. Whose life really touches others and to what extent?

But what an excellent teaching to call our attention to the fact that the world is structured such that our lives impact the greater scheme of things.

As I indicated at the conclusion of the previous chapter, in reading these verses we place humanity at the center of God's intention. Imitating divine resting, neither creating nor destroying for a day, we fulfill the holy purpose of focusing on the spirituality of God's creation. Just reciting these verses elevates the human existential condition to "little lower than the angels." We are not "the human stain" (Philip Roth) or "hollow men" (T. S. Eliot). As we saw in chapter 2, God cares about us directly and includes us in the world's functioning.

What Is Holiness?

What does it mean to "sanctify" or "make holy"? Holiness indicates proximity to God. The holier an object, an activity, or a time period, the more likely it is to intrinsically facilitate access to God's presence. When I was living in Israel we joked about the difference in praying in the United States versus praying in Jerusalem as the difference between a long-distance and a local call. (That was when long-distance calls cost more than local calls and were basically a special event rather than a daily occurrence.) Holiness does not guarantee God's presence. It just increases the odds and removes obstacles. So, the holiness of Shabbat means that we have an increased opportunity to feel God's force in our lives. The same with the other holy times or activities.

In 1969 I was a student at Hebrew University in Jerusalem, living with five other undergrads. The others were Orthodox, and consequently we lived an Orthodox lifestyle. I walked out of my room one morning and one of my roommates was standing with a frying pan in his right hand over our stove, grasping his open siddur in his left hand, wearing tefillin, and davening the morning service. I'm only guessing, but I think that although he was engaged in a holy activity, he was not feeling God's presence. His actual feeling was anxiety at needing to get to class on time, having overindulged in warm blankets.

On the other hand, when Rabbi Abraham Joshua Heschel marched with Dr. Martin Luther King, Jr., in Selma, Alabama, in 1965 he famously remarked, "I felt my legs were praying." Heschel wrote that prayer meant becoming aware of God's presence instead of one's own needs. That's proximity. An intentional act of social justice could create a "holy moment." In praying words attributed to God in a holy place we are more likely to encounter the spiritual. But feeling God's presence can neither be guaranteed nor excluded from possibility. In the final analysis, experiencing holiness depends on the readiness of the individual.

Standard Intermediate Blessing for Shabbat: Drawing Closer to God

Our God and our ancestor's God, accept our rest, sanctify us through Your commandments, and grant us a share in Your Torah. Satisfy us with Your goodness, and gladden us with Your salvation. And purify our heart to serve You in truth. And Adonai our God, lovingly and adoringly grant us as our inheritance Your holy Shabbat, that all of Israel, who sanctify Your name, might rest on it. Blessed are You, Adonai, who sanctifies Shabbat.[2]

We move from the biblical verses for Erev Shabbat to the standard text for each intermediate blessing that we pray in the *Amidah* of every Shabbat service.

Sometimes a single word reference will open a world of symbolism. The Jewish people, as we have consistently said, historically await the restoration of the sacrificial system but implemented prayers that replace sacrifices. Thus, they include both, and traditional prayers make the case that both would be the optimal solution for the future. When the Temple stood, there was a synagogue with prayers on the Temple Mount for the priests, so even before the destruction of the Temple, the priests practiced both prayer and sacrifice.

The Hebrew word *r'tzei* (accept) had been used for acceptance of prayers, but prior to that, for God's acceptance of sacrifices. The verb means "to find favor." It's used to request divine acceptance of offerings from God's people. It brings together both options of human offering to God, oral and sacrificial.

The prophet Ezekiel, a prophet of the first exile, elaborately describes the restoration of the sacrificial system when the people would return from Babylonia. That description of the restored Temple and the dedicatory sacrifices concludes:

> Seven days they shall purge the altar and cleanse it; thus shall it be consecrated. And when these days are over [the dedication of the restored altar], then from the eighth day onward the priests shall offer your burnt offerings and your offerings of well-being on the altar; **and I will extend My favor to you—** declares the Lord God.
>
> (Ezekiel 43:26–27)

The single word *r'tzei*, which we will see again in the first of the prayers of thanksgiving, asks for God's acceptance of rest, implying that rest can be placed before God as if on an altar and given as a gift as part of the covenant between God and Israel. That makes sense given that God provided Shabbat for renewal already in Genesis.

The Rabbis took great pains in several ways to act as though they maintained the sacrificial system. We saw in chapter 1 that Psalm 51 was used to persuade the people that God did not actually require daily sacrifices, that it was a contrite spirit that God desired rather than the daily offering. Here, too, the same word is used to ask for acceptance as though a sacrifice were being offered, but instead it's Sabbath rest. The Rabbis have not by any means given up on restoring the sacrificial system. Nonetheless, Israel's fulfillment of God's commandments is considered a replacement, particularly if both the fulfillment of mitzvah (commandment) and the sacrifices can be offered together. We have parallel systems operating simultaneously, like belt and suspenders, seeking divine acceptance.

How do we know that God desires rest? Leviticus 23 associates rest with all of the biblical holy times, beginning with Shabbat:

> On six days work may be done, but on the seventh day there shall be **a Sabbath of complete rest**, a sacred occasion. You shall do no work; it shall be a Sabbath of Adonai throughout your settlements.
>
> (Leviticus 23:3)

Our prayer lists ways to draw closer to God, and the next two are "sanctify us through your commandments, and grant us a share in your Torah," which we find in the eighth stanza of Psalm 119:

> Adonai is my portion;
> **I have resolved to keep Your words.**
> I have implored You with all my heart,
> have mercy on me, in accordance with Your promise.
> I have considered my ways,
> and have turned back to Your decrees.
> I have hurried and not delayed
> to keep Your commandments.
> Though the bonds of the wicked are coiled round me,
> I have not neglected Your teaching.
> I arise at midnight to praise You
> for Your just rules.
> **I am a companion to all who fear You,**
> **to those who keep Your precepts.**
> **Your steadfast love, Adonai, fills the earth;**
> **teach me Your laws.**
>
> (PSALM 119:57–64)

The word for "share" in our prayer is the same as "portion" in the psalm. But the entire stanza, and other parts of Psalm 119 as well, ask for God to hold the praying person in mind due to allegiance to God's words and commandments.

Appreciating God's Bounty

Our prayer goes on to ask that we be "satisfied" and "gladdened." Jeremiah predicts that same result after the first exile:

> Hear the word of Adonai, O nations,
> And tell it in the isles afar.
> Say:
> He who scattered Israel will gather them,
> And will guard them as a shepherd his flock.
> For Adonai will ransom Jacob,
> Redeem him from one too strong for him.
> They shall come and shout on the heights of Zion,
> **Radiant over the bounty of Adonai—**
> Over the new grain and wine and oil,
> And over sheep and cattle.
> They shall fare like a watered garden,
> They shall never languish again.
> Then shall maidens dance gaily,
> Young men and old alike.
> I will turn their mourning to joy,
> I will comfort them and cheer them in their grief.
> I will give the priests their fill of fatness,
> **And My people shall enjoy My full bounty**
> —declares Adonai.
>
> (JEREMIAH 31:10–14)

In retelling Israelite history to the people who restored the kingdom after the first exile, Nehemiah warns the people by implication of what can occur if they are not sufficiently appreciative of the bounty God delivers. The people received the benefits but are not as appreciative as one might hope:

> They captured fortified cities and rich land; they took possession of **houses filled with every good thing**, of hewn cisterns, vineyards, olive trees, and fruit trees in abundance. **They ate,**

they were filled, they grew fat; they luxuriated in Your great bounty. Then, defying You, they rebelled; **they cast Your Teaching behind their back**. They killed Your prophets who admonished them to turn them back to You; they committed great impieties.

(Nehemiah 9:25–26)

We hear in our prayer not only a pious hope for the future but also an admonition based on past conduct. Beseeching God to accept Sabbath rest and Torah observance as though they were sacrifices, the prayer asks also that this time around we be truly satisfied with God's goodness and salvation, the very shortcomings that we committed in the past and that we prayerfully hope not to repeat. If we commit ourselves to truly becoming God's servants, perhaps God will purify our intentions.

King David pleaded for a pure heart, according to Psalm 51, in the aftermath of his sin with Bathsheba and rebuke by the prophet, Nathan:

> **Fashion a pure heart for me, O God**;
> create in me a steadfast spirit.
> Do not cast me out of Your presence,
> or take Your holy spirit away from me.
> **Let me again rejoice in Your help**;
> let a vigorous spirit sustain me.
> I will teach transgressors Your ways,
> that sinners may return to You.
>
> (PSALM 51:12–15)

David's heirs may well have been symbolically messaging all of their compatriots who had been disloyal to God and were enduring God's punishments. They will also teach the transgressors God's ways of Torah, in order to be restored to their land, as had prevailed in the days of King David, who, like them, sinned, was punished, but was restored to greatness and once again accepted by God.

Introduction to the Intermediate Blessing for Shabbat Morning: Early Will I Seek You

Moses will be pleased with what he received as his portion, when You called him a faithful servant, crowning him completely as he stood before You on Mount Sinai. He brought down two tablets of stone in his hand and on them was written to keep Shabbat. It is also written in Your Torah:

> The children of Israel shall keep Shabbat, observing Shabbat throughout their generations as an eternal covenant. It is an eternal sign between Me and the children of Israel, for in six days Adonai made heaven and earth, and on the seventh day He rested. [Exodus 31:16–17]

Adonai our God, You did not give it to the nations of the lands, and, our King, You did not bequeath it to idol worshipers. And gentiles will not dwell in its rest. You gave it to Israel Your people in love, to the descendants of Jacob whom You chose. A people who sanctifies the seventh day, they will all be satisfied and delight in Your goodness. You loved the seventh day and sanctified it, calling it the favorite of days, in memory of acts of creation.[3]

Unlike Shabbat, the annual holy days listed in Leviticus 23 were set, during the Second Temple period, according to the sighting of the new moon by a court in Jerusalem. God alone sets the date of Shabbat: every seventh day without fail. In Jewish lore, Shabbat is a foretaste of the world to come. It's a heavenly respite from the weekly toil and troubles of living. No matter what else is happening in our lives, we are commanded to rejoice if at all possible.

It's difficult to imagine a better day and not hard to conceive of Moses rejoicing at relaying the good news to the Jewish people that God has ordained a Sabbath for Israel. The opening line of the introductory Shabbat morning sanctification of the day is traditionally interpreted as Moses relishing this task, given to him as the "faithful servant" of God.

In two places in the Torah we see Moses called God's servant, superior to any other prophet because God addressed Moses face to face. The first occurs when his brother and sister, Aaron and Miriam, criticize Moses for taking a Cushite woman as a wife after his divorce from Zipporah, the mother of his children; and the second is the recording of Moses's death:

> And [God] said, "Hear these My words: When a prophet of Adonai arises among you, I make Myself known to him in a vision, I speak with him in a dream. Not so with **My servant Moses**; **he is trusted** throughout My household. With him I speak mouth to mouth, plainly and not in riddles, and he beholds the likeness of Adonai."
>
> (Numbers 12:6–8)

> So **Moses the servant of Adonai** died there, in the land of Moab, at the command of Adonai.
>
> (Deuteronomy 34:5)

The prayer establishes Moses's authority as the basis of what comes next.

> So Moses carved **two tablets of stone**, like the first, and early in the morning he went up on Mount Sinai, as Adonai had commanded him, taking the two stone tablets with him. Adonai came down in a cloud; He stood with him there, and proclaimed the name Adonai. Adonai passed before him and proclaimed: "Adonai! Adonai! a God compassionate and gracious, slow to anger, abounding in kindness and faithfulness, extending kindness to the thousandth generation, forgiving iniquity, transgression, and sin; yet He does not remit all punishment, but visits the iniquity of parents upon children and children's children, upon the third and fourth generations."
>
> Moses hastened to bow low to the ground in homage, and said, "If I have gained Your favor, O Lord, pray, let the Lord go in our midst, even though this is a stiff-necked people. Pardon our iniquity and our sin, and take us for Your own!"

He said: "I hereby make a covenant. Before all your people I will work such wonders as have not been wrought on all the earth or in any nation; and all the people who are with you shall see how awesome are Adonai's deeds which I will perform for you."

(Exodus 34:4–10)

In the Exodus story, the Ten Commandments were spoken verbally first in Exodus 20 and fourteen chapters later written down by inscribing them on two tablets. Moses receives the thirteen attributes of God, listing God's qualities as they are perceived by God's faithful (see "After Repentance, Forgiveness" in chapter 6). Moses prays that God will walk in the midst of Israel, and God responds with the covenant.

There follows in our prayer a citation from Exodus 31, which requires some introduction. Beginning in Exodus 25, as we have seen above, the Torah speaks of constructing God's Tabernacle in the wilderness, the earthly abode of God's presence (see "Return to Jerusalem" in chapter 6). For the next six chapters the Torah describes in elaborate detail the Tabernacle and its appurtenances, where Moses and God met. This becomes God's physical dwelling place on earth.

This critical section, which picks up again after our citation, continues nearly without interruption through the end of the book of Exodus, another ten chapters of Torah. Its three-time repetition of the details consumes 40 percent of Exodus! Yet, we interrupt describing God's spatial place to announce God's temporal location for holiness: the Sabbath. The Torah interjects the more important spiritual location, Sabbath as holy time, twice into the sixteen chapters describing the physical placement of God's presence on earth. The Torah here demonstrates how Israel carries God's covenant and presence with them, more important than the Tabernacle itself, by observing the weekly Shabbat.

On Shabbat We Become the Sign of the Covenant

In the Torah, God establishes three covenants with humanity. Each covenant is attached to a sign reminding us of the message. The first covenant is with Noah, for which the sign is the rainbow:

God further said, "This is the sign that I set for the covenant between Me and you, and every living creature with you, for all ages to come. I have set My bow in the clouds, and it shall serve as a sign of the covenant between Me and the earth."

(Genesis 9:12–13)

The second covenant is with Abraham, with the sign of circumcision:

God further said to Abraham, "As for you, you and your offspring to come throughout the ages shall keep My covenant. Such shall be the covenant between Me and you and your offspring to follow which you shall keep: every male among you shall be circumcised. You shall circumcise the flesh of your foreskin, and that shall be the sign of the covenant between Me and you."

(Genesis 17:9–11)

The third covenant, reproduced from Exodus 31:16–17 in our prayer, is with the Jewish people. The sign of that covenant, made with the entirety of the Jewish people assembled at the foot of Mount Sinai, unlike the previous two covenants, is not something physical like the rainbow or circumcision. Rather, the sign of the covenant is the Sabbath itself, Moses's happy gift from God to humanity. As we rest on the Sabbath, just as God rested in Genesis 2:1–3, and imitate God's behavior, we bring God into our lives. The holiness of God enters human life by our synchronously repeating God's rest and reciting the portion of God's text that reminds us of the covenant bound up in our observance. Israel itself effectively becomes the sign of the covenant between God and Israel by observing God's Shabbat and resting as God rested, while reciting the words that God gives us in making the gift of Shabbat to the Jewish people. The Sabbath will be a "delight" and "the favorite of days."

The concluding portion of our blessing, after the verses from Exodus 31, emphasizes both the gift to the Jewish people and the joy of Shabbat. The Hebrew word for "delight" is actually familiar in the Jewish community, even if not everyone is immediately aware of its meaning. It originates from Isaiah 58:

If you refrain from trampling the Sabbath,
From pursuing your affairs on My holy day;
If you call the Sabbath "delight" [*oneg*],
Adonai's holy day "honored";
And if you honor it and go not your ways
Nor look to your affairs, nor strike bargains—
Then you can seek the favor of Adonai [*titanag al
    Adonai*].
I will set you astride the heights of the earth,
And **let you enjoy the heritage of your father
    Jacob**—
For the mouth of Adonai has spoken.

(Isaiah 58:13–14)

The Hebrew expression *oneg Shabbat* is well known to modern Jews as snacking after Friday evening worship. But it's actually a category of Shabbat observance that includes all kinds of pleasures, including, among other joys, foods and special meals. Shabbat, we find, is among the greatest of pleasures given to us by God to celebrate life. What's more, we are participating in a "taste of the world to come." Holy time approaches the perfection of paradisiacal time once experienced in the Garden of Eden and that will be restored in messianic time. In the interim, we get a taste of God's perfection by celebrating Shabbat.

An Additional Thought: And You Shall Rejoice—*Yismechu*

Those who keep Shabbat and who call it a delight will rejoice in Your kingdom. A people who sanctifies the seventh day, they will all be satisfied and delight in Your goodness. You loved the seventh day and sanctified it, calling it the favorite of days, in memory of acts of creation.[4]

We've already said that Shabbat is the most glorious of days, a taste of the world to come. There is a tradition in the Talmud that if every member of the House of Israel were to keep the Sabbath for one or two weeks, the messiah would come. What a great thought, that we can actually bring redemption of the world through our celebration! There's no overemphasizing the joy of the day.

Our prayer specifically celebrates that joy. We insert the discussion here because these twenty-four Hebrew words appear in multiple services over the course of Shabbat.

Jews have various prayer rites—traditions about which prayers to say when and what customs to follow. Traditions in Poland differed from northern Italy, and northern Italy from southern Italy; and they all differed with Persia and North Africa. With the expulsion of the Jewish community from Spain in 1492, the lands to which the Spanish Jews fled were termed Sephardi, and followed a different prayer rite from the Jews of northern, central and eastern Europe. The Hebrew word for Spain was and is *S'farad*. Thus, the Jews of such diverse locations as the Iberian Peninsula, southern Italy, Turkey, Greece, North Africa, and the Orient are termed Sephardi. In medieval Hebrew, Germany's name was *Ashkenaz*. Thus, the Jews from the other countries were called Ashkenazi. To a certain extent there were different prayer traditions and different Hebrew pronunciations.

The Ashkenazi prayer books have our prayer in the additional (*Musaf*) service on Shabbat, following the morning service. The prayers of the *Musaf* service replace the additional daily sacrifice in the ancient Temples on Shabbat and biblical festivals. Because the entire *Tefilah* that we have been discussing has as its foundational meaning the replacement of the daily *tamid* (continuous) sacrifice, the *Musaf* service is essentially just a repetition of the *Tefilah*. In the Ashkenazi tradition, our prayer comes exclusively in *Musaf*.

But in the Sephardi tradition, the Jewish community recites this prayer in each *Kedushat HaYom* prayer, the intermediate blessing of the *Tefilah*, except during Shabbat afternoon. It's prayed in the evening, morning, and additional Shabbat services each week. The idea comes from Numbers 10:10, which commands the joyous celebration of Shabbat:

And **on your joyous occasions**—your fixed festivals and new moon days—you shall sound the trumpets over your burnt offerings and your sacrifices of well-being. They shall be a reminder of you before your God: I, Adonai, am your God.

(Numbers 10:10)

Sometimes the structure of the Torah is a bit confusing to Bible readers, making it difficult to know what's occurring in the text. In Exodus 18 the Hebrews, having fled Egypt, arrive at Mount Sinai in the Sinai Peninsula and camp there. On the fiftieth day after the Exodus from Egypt—the sixth day of the Hebrew month of Sivan, on which we celebrate the Feast of Weeks, Shavuot—the Hebrews gather at the foot of the mountain to hear God reveal the Ten Commandments. From these chapters, through the totality of the following Torah book, Leviticus, and up through this tenth chapter of Numbers, the Hebrews are standing at the foot of Mount Sinai getting revelation and preparing to journey into the wilderness. According to our tradition, Moses was on the mountain with God for two forty-day periods, descending finally on the tenth of Tishrei, which is Yom Kippur.

As we have already seen above, Moses receives instructions for the building of the Tabernacle in the wilderness in Exodus 25–40, and in the first chapters of the book of Numbers Moses sets up that Tabernacle at the foot of Mount Sinai. Moses builds it and then dedicates the structure and its contents for twelve days, one day for each tribe.

Now they are receiving their final instructions for the journey through the wilderness to arrive at the Promised Land. We are told that God will let the people know with a cloud during the day and a pillar of fire by night when and where to travel. At the opening of Numbers 10, Moses receives a command to communicate with the people by sounding silver trumpets, letting them know when to advance. These same trumpets will be used to announce war against an enemy. And finally, the trumpets will be sounded over sacrifices on joyous occasions, which is where we get the commandment to be joyous on these holy times, as our prayer instructs us.

Look at the Trees: Actualizing the Holiness of Shabbat

Genesis 2:3 says, "God blessed the seventh day and declared it holy." The first appearance of the Ten Commandments in Exodus 20:8–11 actualizes that cosmic account by bringing the holiness into people's lives:

> Remember the Sabbath day and keep it holy. Six days you shall labor and do all your work, but the seventh day is a Sabbath of Adonai your God: you shall not do any work—you, your son or daughter, your male or female slave, or your cattle, or the stranger who is within your settlements. For in six days Adonai made heaven and earth and sea, and all that is in them, **and He rested on the seventh day; therefore Adonai blessed the Sabbath day and hallowed it.**
>
> (Exodus 20:8–11)

We don't sit around and just remember it's the Sabbath, we do things to actualize its holiness. The parallel commandment in the repetition of the Ten Commandments teaches:

> Observe the Sabbath day and keep it holy, as Adonai your God commanded you.... Remember that you were a slave in the land of Egypt and Adonai your God freed you from there with a mighty hand and an outstretched arm; therefore Adonai your God has commanded you to observe the Sabbath day.
>
> (Deuteronomy 5:12, 5:15)

These two commandments, "remember" and "observe" the Sabbath, correspond to its two reasons: to remind us of the orderly creation of the world and the beneficent Exodus from Egypt. Let's combine them now with the citation from Isaiah 58 mentioned above in connection with the morning service and the *oneg* of Shabbat. Be joyous! Why? Because you have a sacred world. Its order makes sense. The world and God are not capricious; there's a consistency and benevolence in the world's orderliness from which you can gain satisfaction with your daily life. You know God redeems the world because God brought you out of Egypt and by implication will redeem you again when the time comes.

When my son was about four years old, I would take him with me to synagogue after Shabbat dinner at home. One evening I was a little late, arriving for worship with just minutes to spare. I was a very "on time" kind of guy, and I just knew that being late for worship was tantamount to confessing in the newspaper my utter incompetence. My son let himself out of the backseat of the car, and by that time I was a few steps ahead. It was already dark, the lights were on in the parking lot, and my son said, "Daddy, look at the trees." I, a clueless automaton on my way to fulfilling my contract but without the soul that it required, responded, "Come on, we're late for worship." My son said, "But Daddy, look at the trees"—at which point I looked, and I saw the light reflected in the leaves and branches, and how beautiful they were, and how I was insisting on missing this precious moment with my son. I was going inside to sing about rejoicing in Shabbat in a community, but I forgot to notice how precious is creation and that we are free to enjoy each moment as masters of our own destiny but also inheritors of the creation given as a gift by God.

Judaism calls our attention not only to the necessities but also to the priorities in life. Liturgy urges us to consider and set out the priorities. But the liturgy competes with other inputs, like work contracts and expectations of ourselves. In that sense, liturgy is countercultural. It urges eternal values and poignant moments on us and begs us to straighten our priorities. If we find that irrelevant, who is to blame, the messenger or the recipient?

The Festival Intermediate Blessing: How Fortunate to Be Jews

You have chosen us from all the peoples; You loved us and found favor in us; You exalted us above all the tongues and You sanctified us with Your commandments. You drew us close, our King, to Your service and proclaimed Your great and holy name upon us.

[*When the festival begins on Saturday night, add this paragraph:*

You made known to us, Adonai our God, Your righteous ordinances, and You taught us to do the decrees of Your will. You gave us, Adonai our God, fair laws and true teachings, good decrees and commandments. As a heritage You gave us seasons of joy, appointed festivals of holiness, and freewilled festive offerings. You made us heir to the Sabbath holiness, the appointed festival glory, and festive offering of the pilgrimage. You distinguished, Adonai our God, between the sacred and the secular, between light and darkness, between Israel and the peoples, between the seventh day and the six days of labor. Between the sanctity of the Sabbath and the sanctity of the holiday You have distinguished, and the seventh day from among the days of labor You have sanctified. You have distinguished and You have sanctified Your People Israel with Your holiness.]

　　You gave us, Adonai our God, with love [Sabbaths for rest] appointed festivals for gladness, festivals and times for joy, [this day of Sabbath and]

On Pesach	**On Shavuot**	**On Sukkot**	**On Shemini Atzeret and Simchat Torah**
this day of the Festival of Matzot, the time of our freedom	this day of the Festival of Shavuot, the time of the giving of our Torah	this day of the Festival of Sukkot, the time of our gladness	the eighth day, this Festival of Assembly, the time of our gladness

[with love] a holy convocation, a memorial of the Exodus from Egypt.

　　Our God and our ancestors' God, may there arise, come forth, reach up, be noted, be favored, be heard, be recorded, and be remembered before You for deliverance and goodness, for grace, kindness, and mercy, for life and peace; our memory; our record; our ancestors' memory; the memory of the messiah, son of David, Your servant; the memory of Jerusalem, Your holy city; and the memory of the entire House of Israel, Your People, on

On Pesach	On Shavuot	On Sukkot	On Shemini
this day of the Festival of Matzot.	this day of the Festival of Shavuot.	this day of the Festival of Sukkot.	**Atzeret and Simchat Torah** the eighth day, this Festival of Assembly.

Remember us, Adonai our God, on this day for goodness. Record us on this day for blessing. And save us on this day for life.

In this matter of salvation and mercy, spare us and be gracious to us, have mercy upon us and bring salvation, for our eyes turn to You, for You are the sovereign God, gracious and merciful.

Bestow upon us, Adonai our God, the blessing of Your appointed festivals for life and peace, for gladness and for joy, as You desired and promised to bless us.

[*On Shabbat only:* Our God and our ancestor's God, accept our rest.] Sanctify us through Your commandments, and grant us a share in Your Torah. Satisfy us with Your goodness, and gladden us with Your salvation. And purify our heart to serve You in truth. And Adonai our God, [lovingly and adoringly,] with gladness and with joy, grant us as our inheritance Your holy [Shabbat and] the festivals, that all of Israel, who sanctify Your name, might rejoice in You. Blessed are You, Adonai, who sanctifies [Shabbat and] the festivals.[5]

The three joyous biblical festivals celebrate the Exodus from Egypt (Passover, Pesach), the giving of the Torah to the Jewish people on Mount Sinai (Feast of Weeks, Shavuot), and the wandering in the wilderness for forty years (Feast of Booths, Sukkot). Just as on Shabbat, the intermediate prayer tells us the nature of the day. It ends with a paragraph similar to the one concluding the prayer in each of the Shabbat services, but the introductory portions are much more elaborate. Unlike on the Sabbath, the same prayer repeats for each service—evening, morning, and afternoon. But because the identical prayer is used on all three festivals, the prayer twice identifies, with an insert, which holiday we are celebrating.

The message of the prayer is very clear: these festivals are given to us by God for celebration. Let's celebrate!

> And now, O Israel, what does Adonai your God demand of you? Only this: **to revere Adonai your God, to walk only in His paths, to love Him, and to serve Adonai your God with all your heart and soul, keeping Adonai's commandments and laws**, which I enjoin upon you today, **for your good**. Mark, the heavens to their uttermost reaches belong to Adonai your God, the earth and all that is on it! Yet it was to your fathers that Adonai was drawn in His love for them, **so that He chose you, their lineal descendants, from among all peoples**—as is now the case. Cut away, therefore, the thickening about your hearts and stiffen your necks no more. For Adonai your God is God supreme and Lord supreme, the great, the mighty, and the awesome God, who shows no favor and takes no bribe, but upholds the cause of the fatherless and the widow, and befriends the stranger, providing him with food and clothing. You too must befriend the stranger, for you were strangers in the land of Egypt.
>
> You must revere Adonai your God: only Him shall you worship, to Him shall you hold fast, and by His name shall you swear. He is your glory and He is your God, who wrought for you those marvelous, awesome deeds that you saw with your own eyes. Your ancestors went down to Egypt seventy persons in all, and now Adonai your God has made you as numerous as the stars of heaven.
>
> (Deuteronomy 10:12–22)

Chosenness: what a blessing and what a curse! Why is chosenness a curse? Because often the Jewish people have suffered the slings and arrows of oppression on the excuse that we haughtily claimed to be special in God's eyes.

But what, indeed, does it mean to call the Jewish people "chosen"? This passage explains the meaning, as part of a prayer that opens with the words "You have chosen us from all the peoples." The book of Deuteronomy lays out the meaning for us.

Jews do not enjoy special status. Rather, we own obligations not shared by other nations. The paragraph opens, "What does Adonai your God demand of you?" (Deuteronomy 10:12).

First is complete reverence and love of God, with the entirety of our heart and soul. But that is very nebulous. What does it look like in a person's life to love God heart and soul? The next sentence further refines the ideal: to observe Adonai's commandments. No surprise here. In the absence of sacrifice, the Rabbis defined the ways in which Jews preserve the covenant, the most obvious and broad of which is to observe God's commandments.

But here we find a reference to the ancestors, as we will soon see, to Abraham, Isaac, and Jacob. Our thoughts return to the promises of being a blessing that we already found in Genesis 15 and 17. Now a new idea is introduced: that Jews are a stiff-necked people, stubborn, and that requires serving God completely and without reward, the expression for which is "to cut away the thickening about your hearts and stiffen your necks no more" (Deuteronomy 10:16). Now the external circumcision that designates the covenant will be accompanied by an internal cutting about the heart, a sincere devotion to performing God's will. But what, precisely, must be followed?

God desires a moral community accomplished by upholding the cause of the fatherless and the widow, refusing bribes, befriending and caring for the powerless stranger by providing food and clothing, rather than the expected acts of praising God and bringing gifts. God demands hospitality, comforting the afflicted appropriate to the time period. As God brought us out of Egypt, we must never forget the deeply ingrained lesson of servitude and employ our experience for the benefit of those who now suffer as we once did.

Separating Holy from Holy:
Distinguishing Sacred Time

We've seen that Shabbat is an intrinsically holy time. Therefore, when Shabbat ends, we distinguish, in a ceremony called *Havdalah* (separation), between the holy Shabbat and the secular week starting at dark on Saturday night.

But what distinction do we make between Shabbat and the first or a middle day of the festivals? The first day is holy, akin but slightly less than Shabbat. The middle days of a festival, called *chol hamo'ed*, literally, "the secular of the appointed time," are also holy but to a lesser degree. When Shabbat ends, to what distinction do we call attention?

We've read parts of this prayer from Nehemiah before:

> You came down on Mount Sinai and spoke to them from heaven; **You gave them right rules and true teachings; good laws and commandments. You made known to them Your holy Shabbat, and You ordained for them laws, commandments and Teaching**, through Moses Your servant.
>
> (Nehemiah 9:13–14)

Where Nehemiah reminds us of the revelation of Shabbat, as well as the commandments, the books of Exodus and Deuteronomy add the festivals:

> Three times a year you shall hold a festival for Me: You shall observe the Feast of Unleavened Bread [Pesach]—eating unleavened bread for seven days as I have commanded you—at the set time of the month of Abib, for in it you went forth from Egypt; and none shall appear before me empty-handed; and the Feast of the Harvest [Shavuot], of the first fruits of your work, of what you sow in the field; and the Feast of Ingathering [Sukkot] at the end of the year, when you gather in the results of your work from the field. Three times a year all your males shall appear before the Sovereign, Adonai.
>
> (Exodus 23:14–17; similarly, see Deuteronomy 16:16–17)

Not only did God distinguish time as separate, but the people themselves God distinguished from the other nations:

> You shall faithfully observe all of My laws and all of My regulations, lest the Land to which I bring you to settle in spew you out.... **You shall be holy to Me, for I, Adonai, am holy, and I have set you apart from other peoples to be Mine.**
>
> (Leviticus 20:22, 20:26)

As we have witnessed previously, if Israel refuses the commandments, she shall lose the Land, precisely what the people seek to avoid by celebrating the holy times that God has given as a gift. To be chosen is to receive special obligations and responsibilities.

The people are commanded to rejoice on the festivals. Deuteronomy 16 is very similar to Exodus 23, but more extensive. Regarding the Feast of Weeks (Shavuot) and the Feast of Booths (Sukkot), here we find rejoicing on the festivals stated explicitly:

> Then you shall observe the Feast of Weeks for Adonai your God, offering your freewill contribution according as Adonai your God has blessed you. **You shall rejoice before Adonai your God** with your son and daughter, your male and female slave, the Levite in your communities, and the stranger, the fatherless, and the widow in your midst, at the place where Adonai your God will establish His name. **Bear in mind that you were slaves in Egypt, and take care to obey these laws.**
>
> After the ingathering from your threshing floor and your vat, you shall hold the Feast of Booths for seven days. **You shall rejoice in your festival**, with your son and daughter, your male and female slave, the Levite, the stranger, the fatherless, and the widow in your communities.
>
> (Deuteronomy 16:10–14)

The classic location of the commandment to observe the holidays is Leviticus 23:

These are My fixed times, the fixed times of Adonai, which you
shall proclaim as sacred occasions.

(Leviticus 23:2)

Ahad Ha'am wrote, "More than Israel has kept the Sabbath, the Sabbath
has kept Israel." The two are symbiotic. The kabbalists understand
Shabbat as God's bride. The sacred occasions are holy times dedicated
to God's redemption of the world and a time for celebration. More than
any other prayer, the intermediate blessings of the Shabbat and festival liturgy are the meeting place of God and Israel, through holy time.
So many have sadly relinquished that vision, relinquishing the distinction that time can be sacred and therefore the eternal hope enshrined
in Shabbat. "A taste of the world to come," the Rabbis teach. What does
that mean? For me, it's the continuous reminder that God's world overflows with meaning and joy if we dedicate our lives to fulfilling God's
vision on earth.

Avodah: Accept Our Prayers and Sacrifices

Love, Love Me Do

Find favor, Adonai our God, in Your People Israel and in their prayer. And return the sacrifice to the Holy of Holies. In favor accept the fire-offerings of Israel and their prayers in love. And may the service of Israel Your People always be favorable.

[*On the intermediate day of a festival, add the following:*
Our God and our ancestors' God, may there arise, come forth, reach up, be noted, be favored, be heard, be recorded, and be remembered before You for deliverance and goodness, for grace, kindness, and mercy, for life and peace; our memory; our record; our ancestors' memory; the memory of the messiah, son of David, Your servant; the memory of Jerusalem, Your holy city; and the memory of the entire House of Israel, Your People, on

On Pesach this day of the Festival of Matzot.	**On Shavuot** this day of the Festival of Shavuot.	**On Sukkot** this day of the Festival of Sukkot.	**On Shemini Atzeret and Simchat Torah** the eighth day, this Festival of Assembly.

Remember us, Adonai our God, on this day for goodness. Record us on this day for blessing. And save us on this day for life.

In this matter of salvation and mercy, spare us and be gracious to us, have mercy upon us and bring salvation, for our eyes turn to You, for You are the sovereign God, gracious and merciful.]

May our eyes behold Your return to Zion in mercy. Blessed are You, Adonai, who restores His divine presence to Zion.[1]

With the destruction of the Second Temple, the Rabbis confronted a mountainous obstacle looming over and existentially threatening the Jewish people: the necessity to maintain the covenant with God through the sacrificial system in a convincing, authoritative way. If they could not sincerely convince Jews of a bona fide replacement for the sacrificial system, the entire God connection might disintegrate. As we saw in chapter 1, they quoted Psalm 51 to demonstrate the subtle alteration that God desired "a contrite spirit," an adjunct to the sacrifices rather than sacrifices themselves. By bowing at the opening of the *Tefilah*, with the first three words, each worshiper could demonstrate contrition before God, together with prayer as acceptable as the sacrifice itself. The House of Israel, praying in a quorum (a minyan) of ten men together, would represent the people before the heavenly tribunal. The verbal prayers became the offering.

The overall purpose of the entire nineteen prayers of the *Tefilah*, or seven on Shabbat and festivals, is to replace the *tamid*, the daily sacrifice. But how could the Rabbis prove that words offered to God would suffice to replace the sacrificial system? Many means were employed, including the *Avodah* prayer. They exploited the nearly identical prayer that was used at the sacrifices, adding a few pertinent sentences, to validate the effective equivalence of prayer and sacrifice.

The key word here is *avodah*, meaning "service," in the sense of both animal sacrifice and words for worship. The same word is used for both! At the conclusion of the intermediate blessings for weekdays, Shabbat, or holy days, the identical prayer would be recited as was offered at the completion of sacrifices. Both, therefore, represent gifts to God.

"Find Favor, Adonai": One Prayer, Many Meanings

The opening word of the *Avodah* prayer in Hebrew is *r'tzei*, which we have seen previously (see chapter 7).

> Seven days they shall purge the altar and cleanse it; thus shall it be consecrated. And when these days are over [the dedication of the restored altar], then from the eighth day onward the priests shall offer your burnt offerings and your offerings of well-being on the altar; **and I will extend My favor to you—** declares the Lord God.
>
> (Ezekiel 43:26–27)

After the sacrifices have been offered, God says, "And I will extend My favor to you," "favor" being a form of the word *r'tzei* with which our prayer commences. It means that God has accepted the sacrifice, just as we are requesting that God accept our prayers. The word usage makes the offerings appear equal. The comments I made in chapter 7 apply here, except that there Sabbath rest substituted for the sacrifice, and here it's the verbal system of prayer in the form of the *Tefilah*. Prayers replace animal sacrifice.

The *d'vir* of the Temple, the Holy of Holies, is where the priests kept the Ark of the Covenant:

> In the innermost part of the House, **he fixed a Shrine in which to place the Ark of Adonai's Covenant**.
>
> (1 Kings 6:19)

The first sentence of our prayer asks for acceptance (*r'tzei*) of the People Israel and their *Tefilah*. This entire set of seven or nineteen prayers makes up the *Tefilah*, and therefore we are asking for the acceptance of the entirety, not just our single prayer. The next sentence cleverly changes the subject while appearing to be speaking about the same thing: "Return the sacrifice [*avodah*; read alternatively: the prayer service] to the Holy of Holies. In favor accept the fire-offerings of Israel [sacrifices] and their prayers [a form of the word *r'tzei*] in love." Thus the Rabbis transform a prayer offered in the Temple over the sacrifices by using the same terminology to ask for the acceptance of the verbal prayers, purposefully confusing the authority of the two mechanisms, sacrifice and verbal prayer. It's genius alchemy!

We have already seen Isaiah call the Temple "a house of prayer for all peoples." God gathers the exiles from all lands, and Isaiah specifically equates sacrifices and verbal prayers in the Jerusalem Temple:

> All who keep the Sabbath and do not profane it,
> And who hold fast to My covenant—
> **I will bring them to My sacred mount**
> **And let them rejoice in My house of prayer.**
> **Their burnt offerings and sacrifices**
> **Shall be welcome on My altar;**
> **For My House shall be called**
> **A house of prayer for all peoples.**
>
> (ISAIAH 56:6–7)

The English phrase "shall be welcome" in Hebrew is *l'ratzon*, another form of the same word for God's acceptance of sacrifice.

"May Our Eyes Behold": Everything Old Is New Again

The penultimate sentence of the prayer delivers the second essential message. Among the functions of embedding Bible quotations in prayers is to demonstrate that "what happened before is happening again." Just as God redeemed Israel previously, so redemption will again occur under the Romans, despite their destruction and overwhelming might. When has that happened before?

The sentence begins, "May our eyes behold." That same phrase appears elsewhere:

> **When your eyes behold** a king in his beauty,
> When they contemplate the land round about,
> Your throat shall murmur in awe,
> "Where is the one who could count? Where is one
>   who could weigh?
> Where is one who could count [all these] towers?"
> No more shall you see the barbarian folk,
> The people of speech too obscure to comprehend,
> So stammering of tongue that they are not
>   understood.
> **When you gaze upon Zion, our city of assembly,**
> **Your eyes shall behold Jerusalem**
> As a secure homestead....
> For Adonai shall be our prince,
> Adonai shall be our king:
> He shall deliver us.
> Then shall indeed much spoil be divided,
> Even the lame shall seize booty.
> And none who lives there shall say, "I am sick";
> It shall be inhabited by folk whose sin has been forgiven.
>   (Isaiah 33:17–20, 33:22–24)

Isaiah obscures the story, but fortunately it's told elsewhere in the Bible: 2 Kings 18:1–20:19, and a great story it is. Let me summarize.

Chapters 18–20 of 2 Kings singles out King Hezekiah, one of just a few good kings of Judah, the southern kingdom in what today we term the Land of Israel. In the fourth year of Hezekiah's reign in Judah, King Shalmaneser of Assyria captures the northern kingdom, here called Samaria, and deports the people to what is today Iraq. We call those people today the ten lost tribes of Israel.

Assyria remains militarily the world's superpower of the eighth century BCE. Hezekiah errs and allies himself with Egypt, and ten years after Assyria destroys Samaria they lay siege to Judea and Jerusalem as punishment. Hezekiah apologizes to King Sennacherib, who has ascended to the throne, and offers to pay tribute to Assyria. In Isaiah that's the meaning of the question about "counting and weighing"; it's to determine the taxes paid to Assyria.

The Assyrian king sends messengers to intimidate Hezekiah's advisors, announcing to Hezekiah that they have been sent by God to destroy Judah and that no one can withstand them. The God of Judea, they say, possesses insufficient power to counter the mightiest nation in the world, and Jerusalem will be destroyed. The Assyrians, ("the people of speech too obscure to comprehend" in Isaiah 33:19), who speak Aramaic to Hezekiah's representatives, address directly the watchers on the walls of Jerusalem in their own language, describing explicitly how Jerusalemites will suffer hunger in the siege. If they will just surrender, they will not starve, but will have "bread and wine, olive oil and honey, in order to live and not die." They say, "Don't listen to Hezekiah, who misleads you by saying, 'Adonai will save us.' Did any of the gods of other nations save the land from the king of Assyria?" (2 Kings 18:32–33).

Hezekiah's messengers trek to inquire of Isaiah, who informs them of God's plans to deceive and destroy the Assyrian army, assuring them that the Assyrians will retreat to their homeland, leaving Jerusalem unharmed.

Hezekiah ascends Mount Moriah to pray to God, where he informs God of the might of the Assyrian army, concluding by pleading, "But now, Adonai our God, deliver us from his hands, and let all the kingdoms of the earth know that You alone, Adonai, are God."

"Your Return to Zion": God Versus Gods

We need to pause and look back for a moment to the Torah. When Israel departs from Mount Sinai intending to travel toward the Promised Land, having spent the thirteen months since the Exodus receiving God's revelation, Moses sends twelve spies into Israel, and ten return with an "evil report." The Hebrews, out of fear, refuse the Land occupied by "giants." God becomes so incensed with the Hebrews that God tells Moses that God will destroy this people and start over, appointing Moses to lead a different people, to which Moses responds:

> When the Egyptians, from whose midst You brought up this people in Your might, hear the news, they will tell it to the inhabitants of that land. Now they have heard that You, Adonai, are in the midst of this people; that You, Adonai, appear in plain sight when Your cloud rests over them and when You go before them in a pillar of cloud by day and a pillar of fire by night. If then You slay this people to a man, the nations who have heard Your fame will say, "It must be because Adonai was powerless to bring that people into the Land He had promised them on oath that He slaughtered them in the wilderness."
>
> (Numbers 14:13–16)

In other words, Israel is God's demonstration project, and were God to appear to lose this battle, God would also lose the entire enterprise of bringing all the peoples to worship God. God dare not risk it. God's got a lot invested over hundreds of years. Moses convinces God not to let God's short-term anger threaten the long-term project.

God responds, "I have pardoned according to your word" (Numbers 14:20).

Again, with Hezekiah, God faces virtually the same situation. It appears that Hezekiah has God over a barrel. Were God to lose the Land, it would appear that God cannot control the world, that other gods are more powerful, and the nations have nothing to fear or any reason to follow God's lead. What will become of God's attempt to bring the nations to worship the one true God?

Isaiah follows Hezekiah's prayer with this message from God:

> Thus said Adonai, the God of Israel: I have heard the prayer you have offered to Me concerning King Sennacherib of Assyria. This is the word that Adonai has spoken concerning him:

> ... I know your stayings
> and your goings and comings,
> and how you have raged against Me.
> Because you have raged against Me,
> And your tumult has reached My ears,
> I will place My hook in your nose
> And My bit between your jaws;
> And I will make you go back by the road
> By which you came.
>
> (2 KINGS 19:20–21, 19:27–28)

Assyria will be forced to withdraw at God's command. Zion, a name used for Jerusalem both in our prayer and in Isaiah, will be saved from the world's strongest military power despite the long odds against it, because Adonai is, in fact, the God who rules the world.

Now let's return to the end of the first century CE in Jerusalem. Jerusalem is occupied by the unassailable, superpower Roman army. They have proved their might. But the Rabbis know that Jerusalem is again inhabited by "a folk whose sin has been forgiven," as Isaiah said. We have prayed in thirteen blessings that God institute God's reign in the world. Or, on a festival or Shabbat, we have celebrated God's holiness in the world. Now all that remains is for God once again to demonstrate God's might and dispatch that overwhelming military power to prove to the world that Israel's God is truly God.

That is the meaning of "May our eyes behold your return to Zion in mercy." A simple quotation recalls an entire historical precedent by which to judge Israel's current reality and expect, once again, God's redemption.

"Who Restores His Divine Presence to Zion": Seeking the Restoration of God's Plan

But our story of King Hezekiah does not quite end there. "Hezekiah became dangerously ill." Isaiah takes the role of palliative care practitioner and forthrightly delivers frightening personal news to Hezekiah, "Set your affairs in order, for you are going to die; you will not get well" (2 Kings 20:1). Hezekiah once again prays to God, in a manner that sets a pattern for later generations of praying near a wall:

> Thereupon Hezekiah turned his face to the wall and prayed to Adonai. He said, "Please, Adonai, remember how I have walked before You sincerely and wholeheartedly, and have done what is pleasing to You." And Hezekiah wept profusely.
>
> Before Isaiah had gone out of the middle court, the word of Adonai came to him: "Go back and say to Hezekiah, the ruler of My people: Thus said Adonai, the God of your father David: I have heard your prayer, I have seen your tears. I am going to heal you; on the third day you shall go up to the House of Adonai. And I will add fifteen years to your life. I will also rescue you and this city for My sake and for the sake of My servant David."
>
> (2 Kings 20:2–6)

Fit this into the prayers we have just recited. The process of redemption ended with the descendant of David on the throne. King Hezekiah, also David's descendant, has two prayers answered to save his land, his people, and the city of Jerusalem because of his righteousness, his pleading, and his ancestor David. The situation almost exactly repeats seven centuries later, and the Rabbis are beseeching God that they achieve the same results: the Land and the city will be saved, and the descendant of David will again occupy the throne. All this we discover by locating the same words as appear in our prayer where they appear in the Bible and reading the story closely.

If the praying person knows the history, he or she cannot overlook not only the promise of national restoration but also the hope for personal healing. Perhaps we have all seen miraculous stories of recovery from illness. I certainly have witnessed spontaneous curative events that no medical doctor could explain but for which everyone gave thanks, like the woman who survived for eighteen years with pancreatic cancer, or the few patients whose cancers spontaneously disappeared. The truth is that we all hope for that, that we be the one in a thousand to recover from this particular grave illness.

But there is yet another aspect: a close friend of mine survived for nearly seventeen years with a disease whose normal course would have predicted that he would be dead in just five years. We might all hope for such healing, but there is more to the story. First, he worked hard at finding the best medical science available. Second, he was willing to endure considerable pain on the road to recovery, without promise that things would indeed get better, but brimming with and inspiring hope. Finally—and this is critical—although he had to forsake his extremely exacting profession, brain surgery, he never abandoned his life. He found new ways to "give back" when he could no longer practice professionally. He lived every day to be a blessing to his world and his family in particular. He taught all of us to live in the moment, but not for the moment. In that, he received the blessing of Hezekiah: to have his life extended, but also to use that time to its greatest advantage, without knowing the ultimate result of his actions or his faith. Thus he lived until he died. The story of Hezekiah, even without Isaiah's promise, can inspire us to invest in life until death claims our bodies, and with the faith that all life is a blessing.

The closing line of our prayer states, "Blessed are You, Adonai, who restores His divine presence to Zion." In a sense, this is the crux of the matter. As we saw in chapter 6, God determined that the Divine Presence, the *Shekhinah*, would live in the Holy of Holies, referred to in our prayer as the *d'vir*, as God's home on earth. But with the destruction of the Temple in 70 CE by the Romans, the command "And let them make Me a sanctuary that I may dwell among them" (Exodus 25:8) would no longer be implementable. Therefore, the Rabbis thought, as a midrash, has it, the *Shekhinah* reluctantly withdrew. Prayer might draw the Divine Presence back to Jerusalem, but restoration would certainly do it, as had been proved by history. We have historical precedent. Utter calamity had been avoided by prayer, and Jerusalem had been restored through the process of punishment, repentance, and return. The prayer asks for God's restoration of the divine plan, which had been dislodged by Israel's sin but for which Israel had repented and been punished. Our prayer, in effect, pleads, "Please, God, restore the order to the world that You intended. We are so very grateful that You chose us as Your people to serve You in the world, and we seek to restore Your divine order so that Your world might be redeemed."

Not only might we experience God's redemption, but personal redemption as well. As my friend created for himself: intention to live as God desires until the day we die will extend our lives to live purposefully, even if we do not live more days. We never actually understand when God will hear prayer, and ours is not to contemplate our personal endtime. Instead, we ask God's will to answer our prayer to live with purpose, and perhaps we, like Hezekiah and my friend, will be granted abundant life.

Hoda'ah: Thanksgiving

We Thank You, the Source of Blessing

We gratefully acknowledge that You are Adonai our God and our ancestors' God for ever and ever. You are the Rock of our lives and the Shield of our salvation from generation to generation. We gratefully acknowledge You by rendering Your praises, for our lives, which are in Your hands, and for our souls, which are entrusted to You, and for Your miracles that are with us on each day, and for the wonders and goodness at every time, evening, morning, and afternoon. You are good, for Your mercy never ceases. You are merciful, for Your kindness never ends. You have always been our hope.

[*On Hanukkah or Purim, add the following:*]

For all of these Your name will be blessed and exalted, our King, forever to the ends of time.

All that lives will gratefully acknowledge You forever and praise Your name in truth, God, our salvation and our help, forever. Blessed are You, Adonai, whose name is good and to whom grateful acknowledgment is befitting.[1]

The final three blessings of the *Tefilah* are called Blessings of Thanks, but in fact only this blessing, *Hoda'ah*, the second of the three, meets the description. Like the previous prayer, the Mishnah tells us that it may well have been said over the sacrifices to express appreciation to God for acceptance. It's well known that psalms were recited over the sacrifices in the Second Temple, and Psalm 92 opens with the following:

> **It is good to praise Adonai**,
> to sing hymns to Your name, O Most High,
> To proclaim Your steadfast love at daybreak,
> Your faithfulness each night.
>
> (PSALM 92:2–3)

Just as with the first prayer of the *Tefilah*, we bow first from the waist, then the knees, and then stand upright in the first and last sentences of the prayer, demonstrating contrition in accordance with Psalm 51:19 (see chapter 1).

The previous chapter proved the mutuality between prayer and sacrifice created by the Rabbis. In the following excerpt, too, the revered King David, whose throne the Rabbis hoped God would restore, demonstrates that prayer and sacrifice are two pieces of a single unit. It's not so much that one can substitute for the other as that both are components showing our gratitude to God for divine bounty to the people.

Notice in the first sentence the standard form of a blessing that we use today, as God is blessed in the personal second person rather than the impersonal third person, "Blessed is Adonai," which is so common in the Bible.

> David blessed Adonai in front of all the assemblage; David said, **"Blessed are You, Adonai, God of Israel our father, from eternity to eternity.** Yours, Adonai, are greatness, might, splendor, triumph, and majesty—yes, all that is in heaven and earth; to You, Adonai, belong kingship and pre-eminence above all. Riches and honor are Yours to dispense; You have dominion over all; with You are strength and might,

and it is in Your power to make anyone great and strong. Now, God, we praise You and extol Your glorious name. Who am I and who are my people, that we should have the means to make such a freewill offering; but all is from You, and it is Your gift that we have given to You. For we are sojourners with You, mere transients like our fathers; our days on earth are like a shadow, with nothing in prospect. Adonai our God, all this great mass that we have laid aside to build You a House for Your holy name is from You, and it is all Yours. I know, God, that You search the heart and desire uprightness; **I, with upright heart, freely offered all these things; now Your people, who are present here—I saw them joyously making freewill offerings.** Adonai God of Abraham, Isaac, and Israel, our fathers, remember this to the eternal credit of the thoughts of Your people's hearts, and make their hearts constant toward You. As to my son Solomon, give him a whole heart to observe Your commandments, Your admonitions, and Your laws, and to fulfill them all, and to build this temple for which I have made provision."

David said to the whole assemblage, "Now bless Adonai your God." All the assemblage blessed Adonai, God of their fathers, and bowed their heads low to Adonai and the king.

(1 Chronicles 29:10–20)

"You Are Merciful, for Your Kindness Never Ends": Our Eternal Source of Hope

The siege and devastation of the First Temple horrified the people, akin to accounts we have today of the Holocaust. The scope was not comparable, but the book of Lamentations records horrors as dreadful as the suffering of our people in our own era. To remind ourselves of such an affliction is also to remind ourselves that God redeems and the people recovers and is restored. It is my own belief that seventy years after the Holocaust we are still recovering, and so we might begin to appreciate the scourge they suffered and the gratitude they felt for their renewal.

Our prayer says, "You are merciful, for Your kindness never ends. You have always been our hope."

> But this do I call to mind,
> **Therefore I have hope;**
> **The kindness of Adonai has not ended,**
> His mercies are not spent.
> They are renewed every morning—
> Ample is Your grace!
> "Adonai is my portion," I say with full heart;
> Therefore **will I hope in Him.**
> **Adonai is good to those who trust in Him,**
> **To the one who seeks Him;**
> **It is good to wait patiently**
> **Till rescue comes from Adonai.**
>
> (LAMENTATIONS 3:21–26)

The final verse of Psalm 79 states that we will sing God's praises eternally (l'olam, "forever"), from generation to generation (l'dor vador, "for all time"). But truly, the entire psalm must have been on the minds of those who watched the heathens lay waste God's holy mountain. The Temple Mount was so engulfed in flame that limestone blocks weighing hundreds of tons exploded and fell to the stone-paved street below. Complete tragedy overwhelmed the nation—spiritual, military, religious, and economic. The Romans decimated the Jewish people.

> O God, heathens have entered Your domain,
> defiled Your holy temple,
> and turned Jerusalem into ruins.
> They have left Your servants' corpses
> as food for the fowl of heaven,
> and the flesh of Your faithful for the wild beasts.
> Their blood was shed like water around Jerusalem,
> with none to bury them.
> We have become the butt of our neighbors,
> the scorn and derision of those around us.

How long, Adonai, will You be angry forever,
will Your indignation blaze like fire?
Pour out Your fury on the nations that do not know You,
upon the kingdoms that do not invoke Your name,
for they have devoured Jacob
and desolated his home.
Do not hold our former iniquities against us;
let Your compassion come swiftly toward us,
for we have sunk very low.
Help us, **O God, our deliverer**,
for the sake of the glory of Your name.
Save us and forgive our sin,
for the sake of Your name.
Let the nations not say, "Where is their God?"
Before our eyes let it be known among the nations
that You avenge the spilled blood of Your servants.
Let the groans of the prisoners reach You;
reprieve those condemned to death,
as befits Your great strength.
Pay back our neighbors sevenfold
for the abuse they have flung at You, O Lord.
Then we, Your people,
the flock You shepherd,
shall glorify You forever;
for all time we shall tell Your praises.

(PSALM 79:1–13)

Various political groups vied for control in the late first century CE, the beginning of the post-Temple period. The Rabbis constituted a small portion of the population who, over subsequent centuries, succeeded in replacing biblical priests, sacrifices, and the Temple Mount with commandments (mitzvot), rabbis, synagogues, and prayers. Psalm 79 expresses so clearly the emotions while the Temple stood. Feel the power and anger at the loss! The Rabbis accomplished a miracle. They didn't invent right there on the spot prayer or synagogue life, nor the literature that explained the transition, Jewish law (halakhah) and Jewish lore (midrash). They developed and grew these new forms over nearly a millennium. But the Rabbis of the first five hundred years of the Common Era seamlessly wove the Rabbinic system into the biblical system, even though they were as distinct as words and animal sacrifice.

Underlying both systems the human spirit remains the same. Even today prayers of every religion can be grouped into the three types: praise, petition, and thanks. The first three prayers of the *Tefilah* praise God. Then come the petitions on weekdays and the proclamations of the holiness of the day for Sabbaths and festivals. The Rabbis brilliantly follow these verbal offerings with three prayers, aspects of which had been used in the sacrificial system. In our *Hoda'ah* prayer, the bowing replicates bowing by the people who ascended the Temple Mount to offer sacrifices and thus was a practice likely known to post-destruction Jews who adopted prayer instead of sacrifice.

In the book of Chronicles we see the blessing formula used as it is used in our prayers, as though the two fit hand in glove, one single tradition continuing from Temple into synagogue. We hear proclamations of God's eternal covenant with the Jewish people that will never be disrupted from generation to generation.

"For Our Lives": Our Gratitude No Matter What Life Brings

All of this is infused with the very human sentiment to thank our Creator for divine kindness in protecting our lives. For no matter what else has happened, if we are aware of our existence, we are alive enough to say blessings of gratitude for life itself. That, then, is the theme of our prayer: our gratitude for our lives no matter what the circumstances, as did my friend whose story I told in the previous prayer, "for our lives, which are in Your hands, and for our souls, which are entrusted to You, and for Your miracles that are with us each day, and for the wonders and goodness at every time, evening, morning, and afternoon." Life itself is a miracle, and we face our beneficent Creator with gratitude, having listed our desires along with the ultimate redemption of the world and the creation of a final Garden of Eden of earthly perfection. The prayers guard us through the struggles of Jewish history and the ultimate desire for an ideal world, which overflows with justice and peace. But this prayer reminds us that our lives are simply in God's hands night and day.

> **As for me, I call to God;**
> **Adonai will deliver me.**
> **Evening, morning and noon,**
> I complain and moan,
> and He hears my voice.
> He redeems me unharmed
> from the battle against me;
> it is as though many are on my side.
> God who has reigned from the first,
> who will have no successor,
> hears and humbles those who have no fear of God.
> *Selah.*
>
> (PSALM 55:17–20)

This is not a national appeal as we have seen previously, but rather a personal salvation, that we find strength and comfort in God's hands. It is just what we require religiously today. Even as we list our image of perfection, we nonetheless thank God for the constant blessings in our lives. And isn't that our existential struggle, to strive to perfect the world even as we sincerely labor to discover contentment with what we have? "Who is rich?" the Rabbis inquire. "He who is content with his portion" (*Pirkei Avot* 4:1).

Israeli Hasidic Rabbi Adin Steinsaltz, sometimes referred to as the greatest scholar since thirteenth-century Rabbi Moses Maimonides, admonishes that we should be tranquil internally with God, but not content toward the world, because of its imperfections. This is the stance of our prayer. God is good because God's mercy pervades the world. But notice that God's goodness is cited in our excerpt from chapter 3 of Lamentations, the most dismal book of the Bible. Our contentment lies in God's perfection; our malcontent should be rooted in the world's corruption of God's goals for humanity.

Therefore we turn to the two holidays celebrated in the course of this prayer: Hanukkah and Purim. When the holidays occur, the eight days of Hanukkah and the single day of Purim, we recite the respective paragraphs as part of the prayer of thanksgiving. Hanukkah celebrates national redemption, as the Maccabees of the second century BCE regained control of the Temple Mount and rededicated the sacrificial system destroyed by the Syrian king Antiochus IV. Purim celebrates redemption from annihilation when Jews live outside of their homeland under foreign sovereignty and are vulnerable to the whims of a foreign ruler. In both instances heroic Jews saved the Jewish populous, one in battle and one with cunning.

Hanukkah Insertion:
From Destruction to Redemption Then and Now

For the miracles and for the redemption and for the mighty acts and for the triumphs and for the wars You brought about for our ancestors in those days at this time of year—in the days of the Hasmonean, Mattathias ben Yohanan, the high priest, and his sons, when the evil government of Greece rose up against Your People Israel to make them forget your Torah and to make them leave the laws of Your will: In Your great mercy You rose up with them in their time of trouble and fought in their fight, judged their cause just, and avenged them with a vengeance. You delivered the mighty into the hands of the weak, the many into the hands of the few, the unclean into the hands of the pure, the evil into the hands of the righteous, and the arrogant into the hands of those who engage in Your Torah. For You, You made a great and holy name in Your world; and for Your People Israel, You brought about a great triumph and redemption on that very day. And then Your children came to the Holy of Holies, and emptied Your temple, and purified Your holy place, and lit candles in Your holy courts, and established these eight days of Hanukkah gratefully to acknowledge, and to praise Your great name.[2]

Antiochus, the enemy in the Hanukkah story, decreed an end to Jewish practices and desecrated the Temple Mount, halting the sacrificial system for three years, until the rededication of the Temple Mount by the Maccabees. *Hanukkah* means "dedication." In our prayer—"when the evil government of Greece rose up against Your People Israel to make them forget Your Torah"—those who composed our prayer tapped into the memory bank of our people. Again from the book of Lamentations:

> The Lord has acted like a foe,
> He has laid waste Israel,
> Laid waste all her citadels,
> Destroyed her strongholds.
> He has increased within Fair Judah
> Mourning and moaning.
> He has stripped His Booth like a garden,
> **He has destroyed His Tabernacle,**
> **Adonai has ended [*shicheit*, "destroyed"] in Zion**
> **Festival and Sabbath;**
> In His raging anger He has spurned
> King and priest.
> **The Lord has rejected His altar,**
> **Disdained His sanctuary.**
>
> (LAMENTATIONS 2:5–7)

The prayer connects the destruction of the First Temple with the Syrian destruction and the Second Temple. The first two were restored, setting a pattern. The book of Psalms lends a timeless quality to events. Certainly within the Jewish world we have a sense of the patterns, including the tragic pattern of oppression and deliverance. We have lived this in our own day with the Nazi destruction. Although historians claim otherwise, in the Jewish psyche the redemption of the people provided by the modern State of Israel follows the destruction to resurrection pattern commemorated by Hanukkah. Psalm 119 uses the very term for "the arrogant" found in our prayer, implying that it is this stanza the prayer has in mind:

Remember Your word to Your servant
through which You have given me hope.
This is my comfort in my affliction,
That Your promise has preserved me.
Though the arrogant have cruelly mocked me,
I have not swerved from Your teaching.
I remember Your rules of old, Adonai,
And find comfort in them.
I am seized with rage
because of the wicked who forsake Your teaching.
Your laws are a source of strength to me
wherever I may dwell.
I remember Your name at night, Adonai,
and obey Your teaching.
This has been my lot
for I have observed Your precepts.

(PSALM 119:49–56)

For modern Jews, the fear of oppression and the hope of deliverance from unforeseeable persecution are overwhelming. The intention of the question "Could it happen here?" does not require explanation; every Jew gets it! I personally believe that many have left Judaism rather than retain membership among a hunted people. The word "arrogant" captures that sense of the infidel who oppresses God's people without reason or warning. It presents the existential anxiety of our age, meaningless death, and therefore a prayer the average Jew comprehends in his or her *kishkes* (guts)!

Some say that Hanukkah resonates with American Jews and is one of the four popular holidays celebrated by nearly the entire Jewish population of North America because of the parallels to Christmas, with its gift giving and the winter solstice. But I add another and, I believe, more profound reason: post-Holocaust American Jewry needs the reassurance of celebrating this victory as a counter to Holocaust fear—"You delivered the mighty into the hands of the weak, the many into the hands of the few, the unclean into the hands of the pure, the evil into the hands of the righteous, and the arrogant into the hands of those who engage in Your Torah." The emotional resonance after the Holocaust, the founding of the State of Israel, and all of Israel's subsequent wars still underlies and guides much of contemporary Jewish life. Even atheist Jews, when they first visit Israel, often feel like they are coming home. I have seen men kneel down on the tarmac at Ben Gurion Airport and kiss the ground they walk on, even if they have never been there before! It's escape from anti-Semitism and persecution. It's the feeling of autonomy and self-definition that inspires cohesion within much of modern Jewish life. Hanukkah conveys the myth and transports us back two thousand years, making Israelis and identifying modern Jews into Maccabees, with different enemies but surmounting the same threat.

Insertion for Purim: Our Part in God's Plan

For the miracles and for the redemption and for the mighty acts and for the triumphs and for the wars You brought about for our ancestors in those days at this time of year—in the days of Mordecai and Esther in the capital city of Shushan, when the evil Haman rose up against them and sought to destroy, to kill, and to wipe out all the Jews, young and old, women and children, in one day, on the thirteenth day of the twelfth month (which is Adar), and to plunder their wealth: In Your great mercy You brought his advice to naught and frustrated his plan. You turned his scheme around on him, so that he and his sons were hanged from a tree.[3]

Both Isaiah and Psalms assure us that God's sovereignty can cancel the will of nations:

> **Hatch a plot—it shall be foiled;**
> **Agree on action—it shall not succeed.**
> **For with us is God!**

> (ISAIAH 8:10)

> Adonai frustrates the plans of nations,
> brings to naught the designs of peoples.
>
> (PSALM 33:10)

We would love the assurance that God will intervene into current events and save us. But, whereas that's the Rabbis' hope, the book of Esther never actually mentions God's name. It's Esther and Mordecai who save the people, with God's role in the background.

Yet, isn't the book of Esther's method the way we should always read history? We have already reasoned that for God to intervene in events supernaturally would seem to argue that God was incapable of constructing a world with rewards and punishments built into its natural laws. Rather, here we see that God's intention is interwoven in history through natural human traits, that Esther has the insight and cunning to foil Haman's plan and that by such means God underlies all of history.

Once again we see a pronouncement of God's judgment on the nations. In a future time the nations will be judged by God according to their treatment of Israel. Just as the conclusion of Esther recounts how the Jewish people wreaked vengeance on their Persian foes, so Joel predicts the same for all of Israel's enemies:

> For lo! In those days
> And in that time,
> When I restore the fortunes
> Of Judah and Jerusalem,
> I will gather all the nations
> And bring them down to the Valley of Jehoshaphat
>   [meaning "God will judge"].
> There I will contend with them
> Over My very own people, Israel,
> Which they scattered among the nations.
> For they divided My land among themselves
> **And cast lots over My people....**

Behold I will rouse them to leave the place you have sold them to, and I will pay you back: **I will deliver your sons and daughters**

into the hands of the people of Judah, and they will sell them into captivity to a distant nation—for Adonai has spoken.

(Joel 4:1–3, 4:7–8)

Obviously, the idea of casting lots to determine the future of Israel is the very name of the holiday of Purim, although the expression for "lots" used here (*goral*) differs from the term centuries later in the book of Esther (*pur*). But the idea carries over, that the nations will not be allowed to determine the destiny of Israel contrary to God's plan.

Finally, we have the fulfillment of the prophecy in Joel that those who plot against the Jewish people will themselves be destroyed in the very manner they intended to afflict the Jewish people:

For Haman son of Hammedatha the Agagite, the foe of all the Jews, had plotted to destroy the Jews, and had cast *pur*—that is, the lot—with intent to crush and exterminate them. But when [Esther] came before the king, he commanded: "With the promulgation of this decree, let the evil plot, which he devised against the Jews, **recoil on his own head**!" So they impaled him and his sons on a stake. For that reason these days were named Purim, after *pur*.

(Esther 9:24–26)

Just as the prophet Joel foresaw, the punishment came not on the Jewish people but on their persecutor, Haman, and his household. But there's an additional insight in the book of Esther. God's role is ignored, as we mentioned. But the insight of Mordecai, the hero of the story, and the cunning of Esther, the heroine, are central to the entire tale. You'll remember that the first of the *Tefilah*'s weekday intermediate blessings recognizes the human ability to distinguish between things because God has given us intelligence to discern differences (see "*Da'at*: Knowledge First" in chapter 6). That quality, built into the world by God, saves the Jewish people through the aegis of Mordecai. When Esther considers whether to put her life on the line to save her people, Mordecai prophetically instructs her:

"Do not imagine that you, of all the Jews, will escape with your life by being in the king's palace. On the contrary, if you keep silent in this crisis, relief and deliverance will come to the Jews from another quarter, while you and your father's house will perish. And who knows, perhaps you have attained to royal position for just such a crisis."

(Esther 4:13–14)

Mordecai and Esther testify to the role divine providence plays in history. It's a sobering thought for our own lives. What role are we, too, playing in local and world history, and what is our role in Jewish history? Are we willingly advancing God's plan in ways we can consciously list and comprehend, or do we do as Esther might have done and refuse, abdicating our role to another person? We may not personally live long enough to comprehend the impact of our lives generations hence, but perhaps the book of Esther is correct in its observation that God has a plan and all of us may well be part of that plan, playing a role on the stage of history that we cannot fully comprehend in our own lifetimes.

Birkat Kohanim / Shalom: The Priestly Blessing / Peace

The Beginning of the End

Birkat Kohanim: **The Priestly Blessing**
Our God and our ancestors' God, bless us with the threefold blessing in the Torah, written by Moses Your servant, and said by Aaron and his sons the priests, Your holy people:

> "May Adonai bless you and keep you.
> May Adonai shine His face toward you and treat you graciously.
> May Adonai lift His face toward you and grant you peace."[1]

Sim Shalom: **Prayer for Peace**
Grant peace, goodness, and blessing, grace, kindness, and mercy to us and to all of Israel, Your People. Bless us, our Father, all of us as one, in the light of Your face, for in the light of Your face, Adonai our God, You gave us a Torah of life, a love of grace, righteousness, blessing, mercy, life, and peace. You see fit to bless Your People Israel at all times, at every hour, with Your peace. Blessed are You, Adonai, who blesses His People Israel with peace.[2]

The Oldest Blessing

In 1979 Professor Gabriel Barkay set out to explore an area on the western shoulder of the Gai Ben Hinnom, the Valley of Ben Hinnom, south and west of the walled Old City of Jerusalem. In a very small archeological dig below the Scottish Church of St. Andrew and behind the Menachem Begin Center (built subsequent to the dig), Barkay discovered a silver scroll containing the oldest quotation from the Hebrew Bible ever found. Stored in the Israel Museum today, it contains *Birkat Kohanim*, the Priestly Blessing, Numbers 6:24–26, which was pronounced by the priests over the people on a stage next to the sacrifices. The amulet was written while the First Temple stood, demonstrating that centuries prior to the final canonization of even the Torah, the people loved these words!

The Priestly Blessing is proclaimed daily in worship in Jerusalem and in Sephardi synagogues worldwide, and during the *Musaf* service (additional service) for the festivals in Ashkenazi congregations. It has several names: *duchenen*, referring to the platform from which the blessing is recited by the priests; *n'si'at kapayim*, meaning "raising of hands," referring to the action of the priests when reciting the blessing; and simply the Priestly Blessing, describing its historic function and authority.

Inserted in the *Tefilah* after the prayer of thanksgiving and connected to the prayer for peace, the Priestly Blessing really is used almost like a prayer unto itself but is not counted in the nineteen weekend or seven holiday blessings of the *Tefilah*. If we think of it as part of the final prayer for peace, then it concludes the replacement for the daily sacrifice, as it was recited at the end of the sacrificial service in the Temple. But the fact that it's used less frequently than the prayer for peace indicates that it has a separate existence from the concluding blessing. Certainly it's a third successive instance of a biblical prayer, previously recited over the sacrifices, being consciously connected to the *Tefilah*. But it's also used by many liberal Jews on other occasions to simply bless the assembled people.

Although the priests traditionally raised their hands in blessing, in my childhood Reform congregation our rabbi, Abraham Shusterman (*z"l*), leading worship robed in his navy blue academic gown with doctoral stripes gracing the sleeves, would raise his hands in priestly manner and bless the congregation to conclude the service. He did not split his fingers as the priests did and do, a sign made famous by Leonard Nimoy, *Star Trek*'s Dr. Spock, who co-opted the idea of the Vulcan Salute from his parents' synagogue. Effectively, the Priestly Blessing was used in my childhood congregation, Har Sinai Temple in Baltimore, Maryland, the way the seventh-century-BCE amulet was used: to ward off bad luck. The liturgical use of the blessing is one of the rare remaining functions for the descendants of the priests, *kohanim*, in modern Jewish worship, as they perform the blessing in the contemporary traditional synagogue. Thus, there are three aspects of the Priestly Blessing: connecting to sacrifice, blessing the people, and a good-luck charm we maintain today.

The Priestly Blessing comes from the book of Numbers:

> Adonai spoke to **Moses**: Speak to **Aaron and his sons**: Thus shall you **bless** the people of Israel. Say to them:
>
> > **May Adonai bless you and keep you!**
> > **May Adonai shine His face toward you and treat**
> > **you graciously!**
> > **May Adonai lift His face toward you and grant**
> > **you peace!**
>
> Thus they shall link My name with the people of Israel, and I will bless them.
>
> (Numbers 6:22–27)

The three-letter root of the Hebrew word *shalom* indicates "wholeness," of which peace is a part. But it's more than simply the absence of war. Obviously, the messianic era that the prayer seeks will be a time of completion, of restoration of the wholeness identified with Davidic kingship. The Priestly Blessing links God to the implementation of this wholeness.

The concluding verse says that through speaking these words to the People Israel, God will bless them. Therefore, the closing blessing of the *Tefilah*, *Sim Shalom*, the prayer for peace, which specifically asks for God's blessing, continues the benediction begun with the Priestly Blessing.

"In the Light of Your Face": Seeking Loving Recognition

In the prayer for peace, we ask for blessing "in the light of Your face," which refers directly to the second and third parts of the Priestly Blessing, which literally mean:

> May Adonai cast the light of His face on you and be
> gracious to you.
> May Adonai lift His face to you and place wholeness
> upon you.

What does it mean for God's face to be toward the people? You only have to consider those you love and what it means either when they smile at you or when they purposefully turn their face away. Babies respond to their mother's faces very early. Lovers look each other in the eyes to feel their presence and share their emotions. We all seek loving recognition by facing one another. Faces recognize presence and confirm existence.

The Torah comments on the same theme at the close of Moses's life. Notice the results of God's turning away God's face from the people:

> This people will thereupon go astray after the alien gods in their midst, in the Land that they are about to enter; they will forsake Me and break My covenant that I made with them. **Then My anger will flare up against them, and I will abandon them and hide My countenance [face] from them.** They shall be ready prey; and many evils and troubles shall befall them. And they shall say on that day, "Surely it is because our God is not in our midst that these evils have befallen us." Yet I will keep My countenance hidden on that day [literal translation: I will surely hide My face], because of all the evil they have done in turning to other gods. Therefore, write down this poem and teach it to the people of Israel; put it in their mouths, in order that this poem may be My witness against the people of Israel.
>
> (Deuteronomy 31:16–19)

Deuteronomy 32 is the poem that follows, but in a larger sense for the Rabbis it's the entire Torah. God turns away from the people as a result of Israel turning away from God and transgressing against the covenant. Disaster follows until the people turn back to God and God restores their well-being, "places *shalom* upon them." The "blessing and keeping" of the Priestly Blessing means that God will place the light of God's face on the people and then be gracious to them, as in the proclamation from Exodus 34, "*Adonai! Adonai!* A God compassionate and gracious ..." (verse 6) (see "*Da'at*: Knowledge First" in chapter 6).

The literal translation of the last words of the Priestly Blessing is "May Adonai lift His face to you and place wholeness upon you." The words are an imperative, that "Adonai should do that," so to speak. Immediately following, the final blessing of the *Tefilah*, the prayer for peace, opens with another form of the same command, taking the concluding idea of the Priestly Blessing and putting it in a different grammatical form, "grant peace" (*sim shalom*). By using the same expression in a different form, "place wholeness upon you" (*v'yaseim l'kha shalom*), the Rabbis establish the linguistic link among the Priestly Blessing, the biblical blessing used after the sacrifices, and the Rabbinic blessing of peace concluding the *Tefilah*.

Peace Looks Like This

The Priestly Blessing contains six verbs, and the prayer for peace correspondingly asks for six different blessings: "peace, goodness, blessing, grace, kindness, and mercy." Not surprisingly, we can cite a biblical quotation for each.

Famously, Psalm 67:2 repeats a portion of the blessing: "May God be gracious to us and bless us; may He show us favor."

Psalm 29, sung in traditional worship during the welcoming portion of Erev Shabbat on Friday night, concludes with a line often used alone as a contemporary Hebrew blessing: "May Adonai grant strength to His people; may Adonai bestow on His people well-being [*shalom*]" (verse 11). The psalm in its entirety speaks poetically of the power of God, concluding with the idea that God is capable of bringing peace to the world. As we have seen from Deuteronomy, however, the people who previously turned away from God must be willing to do their part.

We have mentioned places where divine qualities are listed, notably Exodus 34. But there are others. For instance:

> Let me hear what God, Adonai, will speak;
> **He will speak well-being [*shalom*] to His people;**
> **His faithful ones;**
> may they not turn to folly.
> His help is very near those who fear Him,
> to make His glory dwell in our land.
> **Faithfulness [*chesed*: kindness] and truth [*emet*]**
> **meet;**
> justice [*tzedek*] and **well-being [*shalom*] kiss.**
> Truth springs up from the earth;
> justice looks down from heaven.
> **Adonai also bestows His bounty [*tov*: goodness];**
> our land yields its produce.
> Justice goes out before Him
> as He sets out on His way.
>
> (PSALM 85:9–14)

Thematically, the entirety of this psalm could have been used to complete the *Tefilah*. It pleads with God to remove God's anger, forgive and pardon the people's sins, and restore the Land to "Jacob." What a fitting conclusion, envisioning the process of restoration of Israel to God. It's as though the psalm were written for this very purpose!

Yearning for Yesterday:
Turning to the Source of Blessing

The entire *Tefilah* pleads for God to change the current Roman oppression into a time of Jewish sovereignty, as had been the case earlier, from 142 to 63 BCE. How often do we plead to alter our current reality, to restore it to what had once been? We have all been in this spot during our lives.

Just as in the popular '60s song "Yesterday" by Paul McCartney, our lives may change in a moment, and suddenly yesterday's underappreciated reality becomes today's yearned-for solution. A bad medical diagnosis, the loss of a love, a sudden financial reversal—any of these causes us to bargain with God to reinstate our former situation, whether we valued it at the time or not, and might appropriately motivate us to be grateful for our daily lives and thank God for them, because the one constant in life is change.

God, then, becomes the default source of blessing, even among those who otherwise might not claim to believe in God. So many actually aren't certain what they believe until something goes awry, perhaps validating the axiom "There are no atheists in foxholes." We suddenly turn to the "Source of Blessing," asking for comfort in the anxiety of difficult change.

The Priestly Blessing provides one source that validates God's role in blessing people. But in two other well-known locations we find a listing of divinely ordained blessings and curses, Leviticus 26 and Deuteronomy 28. In Deuteronomy 26, additionally, we find:

> Look down from Your holy abode, from heaven, **and bless Your People Israel** and the soil You have given us, a land flowing with milk and honey, as You swore to our fathers.
>
> (Deuteronomy 26:15)

The idea of blessing is here connected to land, which is the result of heavenly commendation and the people's adherence to God's laws.

Psalm 84 reminds us of God's grace to those who are sinless:

> **Adonai bestows grace** and glory;
> **He does not withhold His bounty** [*tov*: **goodness**]
> **from those who live without blame.**
>
> (PSALM 84:12)

The second part of the verse explains the first, that God's grace is the bounty God gives when in covenant with the people.

God's loving-kindness (*chesed*; "kindness" in the prayer for peace), an extraordinary form of loving that is selfless and the reward of God's grace, is most poetically commanded in Micah 6:

> He has told you, O man, what is good,
> And what Adonai requires of you:
> Only to do justice [*mishpat*]
> **And to love goodness [*chesed*: kindness],**
> And to walk modestly with your God.
>
> (MICAH 6:8)

An accompanying quality in the Bible, God's mercy, compares the compassion God feels for God's people with a parent's compassion:

> **As a father has compassion for his children,**
> **so Adonai has compassion for those who fear Him.**
> For He knows how we are formed;
> He is mindful that we are dust.
>
> (PSALM 103:13–14)

The existential fear of our own mortality comes into play here, that part of God's compassion is for our underlying dread of personal annihilation, disappearing without a trace. In God's grace, God demonstrates compassion, as though the Divine understands that although God is the Creator who put this system into place, God nonetheless appreciates the anxiety our mortality causes.

Torah is equated with choosing life itself. Biblically heaven and earth are called together to witness to eternal pacts, because the witnesses, like God and the Jewish people who are in covenant, must be immortal.

> I call heaven and earth to witness against you this day: I have put before you life and death, blessing and curse. Choose life— if you and your offspring would live—by loving Adonai your God, heeding His commands, and holding fast to Him.
>
> (Deuteronomy 30:19–20)

Clearly, choosing life means choosing God, and we choose God by obeying God's commandments. All of the divine qualities are related in a vision of perfection that arises from a perfect harmony between God's plans and God's people's actions. The divine qualities listed in our prayer come together as complements to one another.

> For the commandment [*mitzvah*] is a lamp
> And the teaching [*Torah*] is a light.
>
> (PROVERBS 6:23)

Torah is often called "light." As a matter of fact, in the other Jewish language of the Rabbis, Aramaic, the word for "Torah" means "light," *oraita*. Wherever light is mentioned, the Rabbis can easily read "Torah" instead. God granting light to God's people, therefore, is the equivalent of giving Torah.

Shalom Rav: The Evening Prayer for Peace

Let it be great peace that You give Your people forever, for You are King and Master of all peace, and You see fit to bless Your People Israel with Your peace every hour and every minute. Blessed are You, Adonai, who blesses His People Israel with peace.[3]

In the evening our prayer opens differently, with a replacement prayer, *Shalom Rav*, which again quotes from Psalm 119:

> **Let it be great peace to those who love Your teaching,**
> they do not have obstacles.
> I hope for Your deliverance, Adonai;
> I observe Your commandments.
> I obey Your decrees
> and love them greatly.
> I obey Your precepts and decrees;
> all my ways are before You.
>
> (PSALM 119:165–168)

Again, our prayer extols love of Torah and the connection between Torah learning and God-given *shalom*. Those who study and observe Torah will know peace.

The Conclusion of the *Tefilah*: Manifesting Wholeness

The *Tefilah* concludes with a biblical account of granting wholeness to God's people, through words performed today as closely as possible to the way they were recited in the First and Second Temples. We connect our lives with our ancestors' and with the biblical vision of covenant. That quality of wholeness, exemplified by peace, results from a series of divine qualities we can manifest in our own lives. But they are interwoven, parts of a wholeness that relieves us of the anxiety of human existence and enables us to choose life, even in our most difficult moments.

This is truly a fitting way to conclude the *Tefilah*, with an ultimate purpose for the individual qualities in each prayer combined into a vision of redemption, the pieces of a puzzle in which the whole is greater than the sum of the parts. Together they deliver a goal for living, a vital connection between mortal humanity and the infinite Divine. We find our purpose and meaning in God's commandments not understood simply as individual tasks, but as a relationship with holiness and a series of actions that, taken together, give human beings a noble partnership, little less than divine, with the Ultimate Eternal Oneness.

Personal Prayer: Reduce My Ego

Smaller Is Actually Larger

My God, guard my tongue from evil and my lips from speaking deceit. To those who insult me, may my soul be silent; may my soul be like dust to everyone. Open my heart to Your Torah, that my soul might pursue Your commandments. As for all who think evil of me, quickly bring their advice to naught and frustrate their plan. Do this for the sake of Your name, for the sake of Your right hand, for the sake of Your holiness, for the sake of Your Torah. For the sake of delivering Your beloved, save with Your right hand and answer me. May the words of my mouth and the thoughts of my heart be favorable before You, Adonai, my rock and my redeemer. May the One who brings peace on high bring peace to us and all Israel. Say: Amen.[1]

We're done! If this were a thousand years ago, we'd have completed the *Tefilah*. We have replaced the twice-daily *tamid* sacrificial offering that maintained the covenant between God and God's people with a series of prayers containing Bible quotations and painting a sequential picture of the process of redemption. But early on the custom was to follow the *Tefilah* with a personal prayer. One particular prayer became the standard. That is the personal prayer of fourth-century Talmudic rabbi Mar bar Ravina. It's my favorite prayer. Here's why.

We all have ego needs. Many years ago I was crossing the threshold of our sanctuary into Friday night worship when an old friend accosted me, saying, "Hey, I heard you dressed inappropriately for the so-and-so wedding. How come?"

Now, first, the wedding was for the daughter of a very close social friend, and an extremely important figure in our congregation. I took great care not to mess up. Second, it was a formal wedding, and I'd worn a tuxedo. Not a lot of variation possible to classify my attire as substandard. The rumor was ridiculous on the face of it. I have no idea why my friend even bothered to say it or why she chose a moment when I was set to lead the congregation in prayer. But immediately I felt someone was trying to make me look foolish. It entirely knocked me off my horse. I felt attacked, blindsided, and vulnerable. Clearly, this was a petty, "first world problem," but I couldn't free myself. In my gut I wanted to strike back.

Although no one could see it, I stewed all the way through the worship. How could such a stupid thing be said about me? I just couldn't get any perspective at all. The comment had captured my soul and was holding it ransom. I was imprisoned by an anonymous force I could not identify, let alone control.

We finished the *Tefilah*, and as always, I read Mar bar Ravina's personal prayer. But this time it grabbed my eyes and affixed my attention. The prayer opened the path to truth: my ego was holding me hostage. Mar bar Ravina opened the jailhouse door. Suddenly I actualized exactly what a rabbi who lived sixteen hundred years ago was feeling. I occupied his head!

In this case we know who in all likelihood wrote the prayer. We've already seen his opening quotation from Psalm 34 in the discussion of the *Tzadikim* prayer in chapter 6, but with a different emphasis:

> Come, my sons, listen to me;
> I will teach you what it is to fear Adonai.
> Who is the man who is eager for life,

who desires years of good fortune?
Guard your tongue from evil,
your lips from speaking deceit.
Shun evil and do good,
seek amity [*shalom*] and pursue it.
The eyes of Adonai are on **the righteous**,
His ears attentive to their cry.

(PSALM 34:12–16)

In chapter 4 we spoke about our ability to rely on God and thereby to direct our own lives. If we allow outside forces to have power over our behavior and our feelings, we'll lose control over our destiny. As a result, we can be buffeted in any wind.

"Guard My Tongue from Evil": The Counterintuitive Way Forward

Psalm 34 speaks of King David and his remorse at failing to rely on God. Scholars, like Robert Alter, explain that this psalm refers to 1 Samuel 21:14, where in a pinch with King Achish, who is here called Abimelech, David feigns madness rather than relying on God for safety. But in Psalm 34:5 he says, "I turned to Adonai, and He answered me; He saved me from all my terrors." Those who revere God will "lack nothing" (Psalm 34:10), and even the strong must rely on God.

At the conclusion of Psalm 34 King David sums up his position:

One misfortune is the deathblow of the wicked;
the foes of the righteous shall be ruined.
Adonai redeems the life of His servants;
all who take refuge in Him shall not be ruined.

(PSALM 34:22–23)

This could have been the theme song of Natan Sharansky in chapter 4 and should have been my refuge in my foolish, ego-crushing experience. We control our fate, not some outside force. But we need to lean upon the strength and faith of reliance upon God. An enemy can manipulate our bodies, but only we direct our spirit.

What is the key to behaving in such an enlightened way? Diminish the ego! I felt vulnerable because I allowed myself to feel attacked. Responding to the attack won't free us. "Guard my tongue from evil," portrays the opposite of what we are feeling at such a moment. It's counterintuitive, yet the only freeing way forward. Direct response will capture you in the snare of engaging with someone who wishes you harm when engagement is not necessary. Let my spirit triumph in humility and independence. It's not an easy lesson but does result from the prayers that went before, in which we learn to rely on God. It's not that evil will not occur. It's that with God's help we can bear it and, more important, forge our own path forward.

This is a very difficult lesson, because we fear the consequences. Yet, to do otherwise is to leave ourselves open to having our lives determined for us. Only we, in coordination with God, can control our spirit. That is the consequence of alliance with God.

"Save with Your Right Hand": Only God Has the Power

Our prayer asks God to save God's beloved people because only God has the power.

> Exalt Yourself over the heavens, O God;
> let Your glory be over all the earth!
> **That those whom You love may be rescued,**
> **deliver with Your right hand and answer me.**
> (PSALM 108:6–7)

The psalm emphasizes that Israel is God's beloved but that we are currently in terrible straits, only to be redeemed by God. The psalm concludes:

> But You have rejected us, O God;
> God, You do not march with our armies.
> Grant us Your aid against the foe,

for the help of man is worthless.
With God we shall triumph;
He will trample our foes.

(PSALM 108:12–14)

What a pious hope. The psalmist reflects their actual reality under Roman rule! Certainly the people feel rejected by God and are pleading for God's return to their aid, for only with divine help will Israel be restored.

Back to the Beginning: What God Truly Wants of Us

The word *ratzon* has appeared before, both in asking that rest be acceptable to fulfill the Sabbath sacrifice and in asking for our sacrifices to connect us to God. It was the verb used to ask God to receive favorably the sacrifice in the Temple. Now it appears again, explicitly requesting that our words be acceptable to God:

May the words of my mouth
And the thoughts of my heart
Be acceptable to [*l'ratzon*: favorable before] You,
Adonai, my rock and my redeemer.

(PSALM 19:15)

The psalm opens praising God's handiwork in creation. In verse 8 it turns from creation to revelation, a praise of God's teaching. These verses are actually an important part of another rubric in Jewish liturgy, the Torah service:

The teaching of Adonai is perfect,
renewing life;
the decrees of Adonai are enduring,
making the simple wise.

(PSALM 19:8)

The entire section is taken by the Rabbis to refer to Torah learning. They conclude with a plea to forgive our transgressions, all of this accomplished by words! Words again replace sacrifices, and we return to the beginning of the *Tefilah*, where Psalm 51 makes it clear that we would offer sacrifices if we could, but God actually requires a contrite spirit expressed through words rather than sacrifices. A crushed heart is synonymous with that contrite spirit:

> True sacrifice to God is a contrite spirit;
> God, You will not despise
> a contrite and crushed heart.
>
> (PSALM 51:19)

Both the prayer introducing the *Tefilah* and now the prayer following the *Tefilah* adduce a contrite spirit demonstrated by a crushed heart to be God's true desire, expressed in words!

> O Lord, open my lips,
> and let my mouth declare Your praise.
>
> (PSALM 51:17)

These expressions bookend the *Tefilah*, demonstrating our Rabbis' conscious conviction of the efficacy of replacing the *tamid* sacrifice with words and Bible quotations. God is the Rock of Israel, and once again, as previously, we see God responsible for Israel's redemption. But not through animal sacrifice as originally; rather, God will desire (*l'ratzon*) the words of our mouths and the utterings of our hearts, because God, who rules on high, redeems Israel.

We conclude on a note of extraordinary humility, with the words of Bildad the Shuhite in the book of Job. Job, of course, suffers the three great afflictions of humanity—loss of wealth, family, and health—for no reason whatsoever. It is the result of a bet between God and the opposing angel, HaSatan (see chapter 2). Bildad, one of Job's friends who comes to comfort him, ends up accusing Job of having transgressed against God when in fact Job is innocent. In our final prayer, we refer to God's abode in the highest heavens, an expression used so frequently today:

> Dominion and dread are His;
> **He brings peace on high.**
> Can His troops be numbered?
> On whom does His light not shine?
> How can man be in the right before God?
> How can one born of woman be cleared of guilt?
> Even the moon is not bright,
> And the stars are not pure in His sight.
> How much less man, a worm,
> The son-of-man, a maggot.
>
> (Job 25:2–6)

After all of these words of exaltation and redemption, are we really going to conclude on such a down note, calling ourselves maggots? At this point, just as we bowed at the beginning of the *Tefilah*, now, when we say, "May the One who brings peace on high," we take three steps backward, followed by three steps forward, and bow to God in humility, about to depart from the Divine Presence. Again we see the parallel with the opening of the *Tefilah*, the contrite spirit and humble posture before God, Creator of all. Indeed, these may be the most perfect words with which to conclude, because God desires a contrite spirit even more than sacrifice. What could be a greater expression of the humble spirit of Israel than the words of Bildad the Shuhite? It's as if we say, "God, acknowledging we are dust, redeem Your people and restore us to the glory of old."

12

What the Words of Prayer Mean to Me

Raise your hand if in junior or senior high school you said these words: "Just tell me if this is going to be on the test," or "Just tell me what it means."

I was a math guy, not an English guy—left brain only. Everything should be part of a formula, and every equation had one right answer. It confused me when we were asked to interpret poetry. "What do you mean you can't tell me exactly what it means? You're going to test me on what it means, right? Tell me what it means." That's what the voice in my head recited every time we had to read a poem or a short story.

But life's not that way, is it? Words have multiple meanings and may point to something very important in our lives, but unshared and not entirely defined. Reading in the prayer book, "May the time not be distant, O God, when Your name shall be worshiped in all the earth ...," reminds me nostalgically of Friday nights in my childhood, sitting in the old Har Sinai Temple ersatz sanctuary on Park Heights Avenue in Baltimore with my parents. But few others would have that memory. Meaning may be very individual, not shared with anyone else.

Or perhaps a word reminds us of an experience we had or even a group memory. Americans are linked by a remembrance of 9/11, even as the story touched each of us individually as well. Jews of a certain age share memories of Israel's Six-Day War in 1967 and Operation Entebbe in 1976. They are historic events etched into our minds, which may

185

evoke particular emotions, which then may create sympathetic ties to other members of our people.

Jewish prayers are a way to speak to God in what Jewish tradition considers God's own language, the words of the Bible. But they are also meant to evoke group memories and ideas in those Jews who pray the words to God. Years ago an elderly man who had just been moved to our community by his daughter had a stroke, and I went to visit him in the hospital. I spoke to him for twenty minutes without him showing a sign that he knew I was in the room or that he was hearing me. He looked straight ahead and never responded. Finally I said to him, "I am going to recite the *Shema* prayer. If you'd like to say it with me, please do." And I started, "*Shema Yisrael*," and here he joined with me, "*Adonai Eloheinu Adonai echad.*" "So," I concluded, "he heard me!" I left soon after and called his daughter from my car. I told her the story. "Mark," she replied, "he hasn't spoken for three weeks, since the stroke. They said he'd never speak again."

I don't know what sensitivities the *Shema* evoked, but they reached deep into his psyche and were powerful enough to get him to talk, a bucket to raise reviving water from memory's wells. Certainly these recollections were contained within communal experiences and perhaps also individual experiences that continued to live inside of him for ninety years. They are like a treasure chest within our psyches, waiting to be opened if we can unearth them and find the proper key. He continued speaking, until he died several weeks later after another stroke.

When I told this story to another rabbi, he said, "Oh, that's happened many times." Whether or not it has, clearly Jews experience something both private and communal by reciting well-known prayers like the *Shema*. They not only communicate something to God, but they communicate a special message within us as well.

What is our situation in life? Have we been in this existential place before? As I write this, the country debates presidential candidate Donald Trump's statement that he wants to exclude Muslims from entering the United States until the government figures out what is going on with terrorism. I know many Jews whose thoughts went right to the Holocaust, just as many Japanese Americans were reminded of their historical experience of being interned on the West Coast of the United States during World War II. The same reference triggered two different group memories. Words have referential meanings to events that are both private and collective. They may vent ideas or emotions that were first experienced long ago. What does it mean to me to be persecuted? Many of my friends were returned in their minds to stories their parents told of surviving the Holocaust. These stories were not their own body's experience, but they evoked overwhelmingly impactful remembrances of the effect of those experiences in their parents' lives and subsequently in their own lives when the events were painfully retold by their parents. Words can wallop us like a tidal wave with their storehouse of emotions.

We have looked primarily at a set of prayers intended to replace the daily national sacrifice offered on behalf of all the Jewish people at least twice a day, with additional sacrifices on Sabbaths and holidays. That system maintained the Jewish contract with God for over a millennium and somehow had to be replaced or its disappearance cogently explained after the destruction of the Second Temple in 70 CE. The early Rabbis equated the sacrifice with a contrite spirit, then demonstrated that the contrite spirit could be displayed before God in the words of prayer. They used the series of prayers to outline the process God would follow to return God's presence to the Temple Mount and restore the Jewish people through the Davidic dynasty. This description, vastly different from the actual sacrificial cult, was equated with the cult through creatively employing biblical citations. The plausibility and virtual guarantee that God would restore God's people was demonstrated by historical parallels in which God had previously punished the people for their sins, but they had been restored and God's presence maintained among God's people.

What does the destruction of the Second Temple mean in the lives of Jews of the first few centuries CE and, more important, to the modern Jew? What does the idea of Jewish destruction and redemption mean in both our personal and our communal lives? When the Jews of the first millennium read Isaiah, they may have thought of their own situation, just as when we read those prayers and quotations we remember the historical events of Jewish communal history but are impacted by the emotions experienced in our own lives. The siddur, particularly the *Tefilah* we have examined here, is meant to facilitate creating contemporary meaning by attaching us to interpretations that we fashion by combining prayers containing our people's history with our personal histories and the events of our day-to-day lives.

But there is even more to the impact of biblical quotations embedded in prayers. So many of us were raised with the idea that prayers are pleadings with God for something special, something particular, and if we don't get that thing that we requested, the prayer was unheard and did not work, causing doubt about God's existence and the efficacy of prayer. But here we find an entirely different import to the process of prayer.

Humans require meaning in our lives. We cannot function without some intuition that our lives make sense on a higher level, that our actions, and therefore our lives, have significance. Perhaps that significance is simply to maintain life for another day. But, for instance, we don't just eat because of instinct and hunger. We eat, in part, as a social experience that creates meaning in our lives through our interactions with those whose cooperation is essential to our well-being. And so it is for all of our actions.

Redemption is the result of the act of providing importance in our lives. Originally what we meant by redemption was that God would provide a better place for us, a world to come after this one, an afterlife in which all of our deeds would be rewarded or punished, and we would experience continued existence to our consciousness. After that time, God would send a messiah to redeem the entire world, and that would provide utopian perfection to all existence, all of the nations of the world. The good will be rewarded and the wicked punished.

But when you think about it, there is a less grandiose idea of redemption as well: that we act for some greater purpose in our lives. For instance, altruistic actions, giving to others without regard to self, provides us with significance beyond our mere personal existence. It connects us to other people and the ideal of goodness. These help motivate us to live with positive intention, and therefore to have a meaning that makes sense to us. In that way all of our lives attain ultimacy and direction, what we might call a telos, even though it may not be national or afterlife oriented. It nonetheless provides a reason to continue living.

In this sense, the prayer book locates our lives in the greater context of Jewish tradition and in the dialogue with God. We don't necessarily have to have answers to prayers. We see our own existential problems reflected in prior situations confronted by our people and the resolution of their problems. The Jewish people is a story that has continued for four thousand years, two-thirds of human recorded history, and we have not only survived but also flourished. Identifying ourselves in the prayers situates us diachronically in that narrative and says to us that no matter how dismal things may sometimes seem, we are part of a larger existence that matters, that impacts humanity, that possesses a purpose, and that will survive despite all odds. They combine to help us contemplate essential existential questions we are living today. History reconstituted in prayer shows us that.

In addition, we find our personal situations reflected in these words, and with contemplation perhaps we will discover a direction. The Hanukkah story of Hannah and her seven sons forced me, as a child, to contemplate my response if someone attempted to compel me to deny my Judaism. Those thoughts, which truly bothered me for quite some time before my tenth birthday, I think played a role in my teenage decision that if I were going to be Jewish, I was going to be the best Jew I could be. Obviously, that idea found a place in my decision to enter the rabbinate and ultimately, if you think about it, in my decision to write the words you are reading. So stories touch our lives. We live out our narratives often in ways we do not examine sufficiently to understand their overall impact. But used properly, the prayers enable us to find a resolution to some of our most personal dilemmas, the situations that force us to search for meaning.

The prayers that we sometimes think of as repetitious and boring actually can compel important dialogues in our lives. Conversations between ourselves and God, between ourselves and Jewish history, between ourselves and the community, and internal to ourselves all take place within the dynamics of the prayers, if we know that they are a possibility and develop them. Jewish prayers contain an often unrecognized vitality that will enable Jews to position ourselves in the world by developing a more powerful and defined identity, a relationship with God and our people, and therefore a clearer destiny for ourselves and those whose lives we touch.

Y'h'yu l'ratzon imrei fee ...

May the words of my mouth, and the mediations of my heart, be acceptable before You, Lord, my rock, and my redeemer.

Notes

Chapter 1: *Adonai Sefatai*

1. Adapted from the translation by Joel M. Hoffman in *My People's Prayer Book*, vol. 2, *The Amidah*, ed. Lawrence A. Hoffman (Woodstock, VT: Jewish Lights, 1998), 51.

Chapter 2: *Adon Olam*

1. Translation from *My People's Prayer Book*, vol. 5, *Birkhot Hashachar* (Morning Blessings), ed. Lawrence A. Hoffman (Woodstock, VT: Jewish Lights, 2001), 93.

Chapter 3: *Avot*

1. Adapted from the translation by Joel M. Hoffman in *My People's Prayer Book*, vol. 2, *The Amidah*, ed. Lawrence A. Hoffman, 57.

Chapter 4: *Gevurot*

1. Adapted from the translation by Joel M. Hoffman in *My People's Prayer Book*, vol. 2, *The Amidah*, ed. Lawrence A. Hoffman, 57–58.
2. Henry Kamm, "Schraransky Tells How He Clung to Psalms Captors Tried to Seize," *New York Times*, February 13, 1986, www.nytimes.com /1986/02/13/world/schraransky-tells-how-he-clung-to-psalms-captors-tried-to-seize.html.
3. *Chumash with Rashi's Commentary*, vol. 1, ed. A. M. Silberman (Jerusalem: Routledge and Kegan Paul,1985).

Chapter 5: *Kedushah*

1. Adapted from the translation by Joel M. Hoffman in *My People's Prayer Book*, vol. 2, *The Amidah*, ed. Lawrence A. Hoffman, 59.
2. Abraham Joshua Heschel, "No Religion Is an Island," in *Moral Grandeur and Spiritual Audacity: Essays*, ed. Susannah Heschel (New York: Farrar, Straus and Giroux, 1996), 262–63.

Chapter 6: The Thirteen Weekday Blessings

1. Adapted from the translation by Joel M. Hoffman in *My People's Prayer Book*, vol. 2, *The Amidah*, ed. Lawrence A. Hoffman, 95.
2. Ibid.
3. Ibid.
4. Ibid.
5. Ibid., 96.
6. Ibid.
7. Ibid., 96–97.
8. Stan Goodenough, "Katrina—The Fist of God?," *Jerusalem Newswire*, August 29, 2005, quoted in Stephen Spector, *Evangelicals and Israel: The Story of American Christian Zionism* (New York: Oxford University Press, 2009), 154–55.
9. "Pastor John Hagee on Christian Zionism," NPR, September 18, 2006, www.npr.org/templates/story/story.php?storyId=6097362.
10. Adapted from the translation by Joel M. Hoffman in *My People's Prayer Book*, vol. 2, *The Amidah*, ed. Lawrence A. Hoffman, 97.
11. Ibid.
12. Ibid.
13. Lawrence A. Hoffman, in *My People's Prayer Book*, vol. 2, *The Amidah*, ed. Lawrence A. Hoffman, 133.
14. Moshe Hayyim Bloch, *Heichal le'divrei Chazal u-Pitgameyhem* (New York: Pardes Publishing House and Shoulson Press, 1948).
15. Manny Fernandez, "Lessons on Love, from a Rabbi Who Knows Hate and Forgiveness," *New York Times*, January 4, 2009, www.nytimes.com/2009/01/05/nyregion/05rabbi.html?_r=0.
16. Adapted from the translation by Joel M. Hoffman in *My People's Prayer Book*, vol. 2, *The Amidah*, ed. Lawrence A. Hoffman, 98.
17. Ibid.
18. Ibid.
19. Arnold Eisen, "Roundtable on Yossi Beilin's *The Death of the American Uncle*: A Review," *Israel Studies* 5, no. 1 (Spring 2000): 343–47; citing Chaim I Waxman, "The Uganda Plan was resoundingly defeated at the Seventh Zionist Congress, but, Beilin suggests, were Herzl's to have won, European Jewry might have escaped the decimation of the Holocaust," in "The Questions Are Much Better Than the Answers," *Israel Studies* 5, no. 1 (Spring 2000): 361–64.
20. Hoffman, *My People's Prayer Book*, vol. 2, *The Amidah*, 99.

Chapter 7: The Intermediate Blessings for Shabbat and Festivals

1. Adapted from the translation by Joel M. Hoffman in *My People's Prayer Book*, vol. 9, *Welcoming the Night:* Minchah *and* Ma'ariv *(Afternoon and Evening Prayer)*, ed. Lawrence A. Hoffman (Woodstock, VT: Jewish Lights, 2005), 121.
2. Ibid.
3. Adapted from the translation by Joel M. Hoffman in *My People's Prayer Book*, vol. 10, *Shabbat Morning:* Shacharit *and* Musaf *(Morning and Additional Services)*, ed. Lawrence A. Hoffman (Woodstock, VT: Jewish Lights, 2007), 105.
4. Ibid., 132.
5. Adapted from the translation by Joel M. Hoffman in *My People's Prayer Book*, vol. 2, *The Amidah*, ed. Lawrence A. Hoffman, 149–50; and *The ArtScroll Siddur*, trans. Nosson Scherman, Rabbinical Council of America edition (Brooklyn, NY: Mesorah, 1987), 665, 667.

Chapter 8: *Avodah*

1. Adapted from the translation by Joel M. Hoffman in *My People's Prayer Book*, vol. 2, *The Amidah*, ed. Lawrence A. Hoffman, 149–50; and *The ArtScroll Siddur*, 667.

Chapter 9: *Hoda'ah*

1. Adapted from the translation by Joel M. Hoffman in *My People's Prayer Book*, vol. 2, *The Amidah*, ed. Lawrence A. Hoffman, 152.
2. Ibid., 151.
3. Ibid., 151–52.

Chapter 10: *Birkat Kohanim / Shalom*

1. Adapted from the translation by Joel M. Hoffman in *My People's Prayer Book*, vol. 2, *The Amidah*, ed. Lawrence A. Hoffman, 152–53.
2. Ibid., 153.
3. Adapted from the translation by Joel M. Hoffman in *My People's Prayer Book*, vol. 9, *Welcoming the Night:* Minchah *and* Ma'ariv *(Afternoon and Evening Prayer)*, ed. Lawrence A. Hoffman, 131.

Chapter 11: Personal Prayer

1. Adapted from the translation by Joel M. Hoffman in *My People's Prayer Book*, vol. 2, *The Amidah*, ed. Lawrence A. Hoffman, 185.

Suggestions for Further Reading

Boyarin, Daniel. *Intertextuality and the Reading of Midrash*. Bloomington, IN: Indiana University Press, 1994.

Elbogen, Ismar. *Jewish Liturgy: A Comprehensive History*, trans. Raymond P. Scheindlin. Philadelphia: The Jewish Publication Society, 1993.

Hammer, Reuven. *Entering Jewish Prayer: A Guide to Personal Devotion and the Worship Service*. New York: Schocken Books, 1994.

Harlow, Jules. *Pray Tell: A Hadassah Guide to Jewish Prayer*. Woodstock, VT: Jewish Lights, 2003.

Hoffman, Lawrence A., ed. *My People's Prayer Book*. Vols. 1–10. Woodstock, VT: Jewish Lights, 1998–2007.

———. *The Way Into Jewish Prayer*. Woodstock, VT: Jewish Lights, 2000.

Kugel, James L., ed. *Prayers That Cite Scripture*. Cambridge, MA: Harvard University Press, 2006.

Nulman, Macy. *The Encyclopedia of Jewish Prayer*. Northvale, NJ: Jason Aronson, 1993.

Reif, Stefan C. *Judaism and Hebrew Prayer*. Cambridge, UK: Cambridge University Press, 1993.

Steinzaltz, Adin. *HaSiddur v'HaT'filah: Madrikh LaM'ayein u-L'mitpalel*. Vol. 1. Tel Aviv: Yediyot Aharonot, 1994.

About Jewish Lights

People of all faiths and backgrounds yearn for books that attract, engage, educate, and spiritually inspire.

Our principal goal is to stimulate thought and help all people learn about who the Jewish People are, where they come from, and what the future can be made to hold. While people of our diverse Jewish heritage are the primary audience, our books speak to people in the Christian world as well and will broaden their understanding of Judaism and the roots of their own faith.

We bring to you authors who are at the forefront of spiritual thought and experience. While each has something different to say, they all say it in a voice that you can hear.

Our books are designed to welcome you and then to engage, stimulate, and inspire. We judge our success not only by whether or not our books are beautiful and commercially successful, but by whether or not they make a difference in your life.

For your information and convenience, at the back of this book we have provided a list of other Jewish Lights books you might find interesting and useful. They cover all the categories of your life:

Bar/Bat Mitzvah	Life Cycle
Bible Study / Midrash	Meditation
Children's Books	Men's Interest
Congregation Resources	Parenting
Current Events / History	Prayer / Ritual / Sacred Practice
Ecology / Environment	Social Justice
Fiction: Mystery, Science Fiction	Spirituality
Grief / Healing	Theology / Philosophy
Holidays / Holy Days	Travel
Inspiration	Twelve Steps
Kabbalah / Mysticism / Enneagram	Women's Interest

Stuart M. Matlins, Publisher

Or phone, fax, mail or email to: **JEWISH LIGHTS Publishing**
Sunset Farm Offices, Route 4 • P.O. Box 237 • Woodstock, Vermont 05091
Tel: (802) 457-4000 • Fax: (802) 457-4004 • www.jewishlights.com
Credit card orders: **(800) 962-4544** (8:30AM–5:30PM EST Monday–Friday)
Generous discounts on quantity orders. SATISFACTION GUARANTEED. Prices subject to change.

For more information about each book, visit our website at www.jewishlights.com.